Six Easy Patterns

FOR WOMEN ONLY

By Martha Campbell Pullen, Ph.D.

May God Bless You

Martha Pullen

Garments featured on

Series 1500 and 1600

Martha Pullen™ Company
149 Old Big Cove Road
Brownsboro, AL 35741
(256)533-9586 • FAX (256)533-9630 • (800) 547-4176 (ext. 2)
Please visit our website at www.marthapullen.com
To receive a free weekly email newsletter, go to www.marthapullen.com and sign up today!

Table of Contents

Editors
Martha Pullen, Kathy McMakin,
Charlotte Potter, Dody Baker, Patty Smith
Claudia Newton, Karen Hinshaw

Garment Design
Sue Pennington, Eileen Roche, Marlis Bennett,
Carol Ingram, Joyce Drexler, Lindee Goodall,
Linnette Whicker, Lana Bennett, June Mellinger,
Connie Palmer, Peggy Dilbone, Patti Jo Larson,
Coni Martin, Pam Mahshie,
Beverley Sheldrick, Kathy Neal

Photography
Jennifer & Company

Book Designer
Laura Beth Yates

Illustrators
Kris Broom, Angela Cataldo Pullen

Martha Pullen Company, Inc.
149 Old Big Cove Road • Brownsboro, AL 35741 • Phone (256)533-9586 • Fax (256)533-9630
www.marthapullen.com • info@marthapullen.com

ISBN: 1-878048-31-7

Tank - General Directions

Unlined Tank with Bias Facing

Supplies

- 45" fabric with or without nap
  XS - SM = 1-1/8 yards
  MD = 1-3/4 yards
  LG - 4XL = 1-7/8 yards
- 60" fabric with or without nap
  XS - SM = 1-1/8 yards
  MD - XL = 1-1/4 yards
  2XL - 4XL – 1-7/8 yards
- Thread to match the fabric
- Basic sewing supplies
- 1/2" bias tape maker

Pattern Pieces

- Tank Front
- Tank Back

Cutting the Pieces

(refer to the layout)

- One front on the fold—remove 3/8" seam allowance from the neck edge and armhole edge after cutting **(fig. 1a)**
- One back on the fold—remove 3/8" seam allowance from the neck edge and armhole edge after cutting **(fig. 1b)**
- Cut enough bias 1" wide to go around the neck and the two armholes
- Mark the darts in the tank front if desired

* All seams are 5/8" unless otherwise noted. To finish seam, trim seam to 1/4" and overcast edge by machine or serger.

—Construction—

1. Stitch bias strips together to make one continuous length of bias **(fig. 2a and 2b)**.
2. Stitch the optional fit darts in the tank front if desired **(fig. 3)**.
3. With right sides together stitch the shoulder seams **(fig. 4)**.
4. Press the bias tape following the instructions included with the bias tape maker.

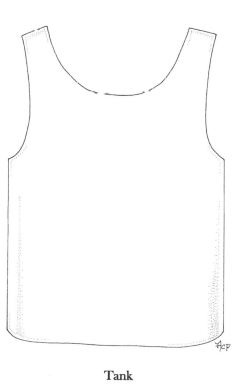

Tank

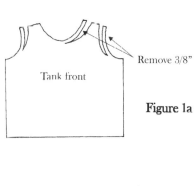

Tank front

Remove 3/8"

Figure 1a

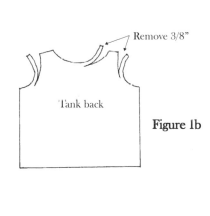

Remove 3/8"

Tank back

Figure 1b

Join bias strips

Figure 2a

Figure 2b

Optional dart

Right side front

Figure 3

Stitch shoulder seams

Wrong side front

Figure 4

5. Unfold one side of the bias tape and pin right sides together along the neck edge beginning at the center back with the end folded back and matching the raw edges of the bias tape and the raw edges of the tank neck edge *(fig. 5)*.

6. Stitch the bias tape to the tank in the unfolded crease of the tape (approximately 1/4"). Clip the seam allowance *(fig. 6)*. Press the facing and seam allowance away from the garment.

7. Understitch the bias facing through the seam *(fig. 7)*. Press the bias facing to the wrong side.

8. Stitch the facing in place along the bottom close to the folded edge of the bias strip *(fig. 8)*.

9. Stitch and finish the side seam *(fig. 9)*.

10. Stitch the bias facing to the armholes with a 1/4" seam in the same manner: starting at the side seam, stitch around the curve back to the side seam *(fig. 10)*.

11. Clip the seam. Press the facing and seam allowance away from the armhole. Understitch the bias facing through the bias and seam close to the seam line *(fig. 11)*.

12. Press the bias facing to the wrong side.

13. Stitch the facing in place close to the folded edge of the bias strip *(fig. 12)*.

14. Hem the bottom of the tank by pressing 1/8" to the wrong side. Then turn up 1/4" to the wrong side and stitch in place *(fig. 13)*.

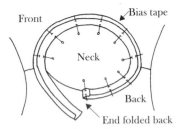

Front — Bias tape — Neck — Back — End folded back

Figure 5

Stitch 1/4" and clip — Back

Figure 6

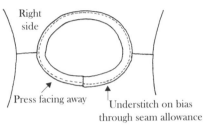

Right side — Press facing away — Understitch on bias through seam allowance

Figure 7

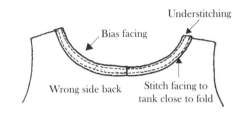

Understitching — Bias facing — Wrong side back — Stitch facing to tank close to fold

Figure 8

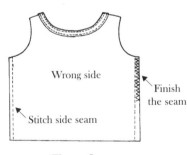

Wrong side — Finish the seam — Stitch side seam

Figure 9

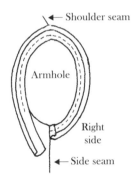

Shoulder seam — Armhole — Right side — Side seam

Figure 10

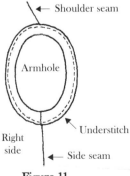

Shoulder seam — Armhole — Understitch — Right side — Side seam

Figure 11

Stitch armhole bias facing — Wrong side

Figure 12

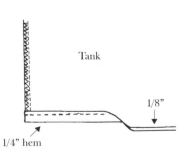

Tank — 1/8" — 1/4" hem

Figure 13

Tank — Lined Version

Supplies

- Refer to fabric requirements for tank with bias facings
- Purchase the same amount of fabric for the lining
- Thread to match the fabric
- Basic sewing supplies

Pattern Pieces

- Tank Front
- Tank Back

* All seams are 5/8" unless otherwise noted. To finish seam, trim seam to 1/4" and overcast edge by machine or serger.

Cutting the Pieces

(refer to the layout)

- Cut one front and one back on the fold from the tank fabric
- Cut one front and one back on the fold from the lining fabric
- Mark the optional darts in both the tank fabric and the lining fabric if desired

—Construction—

1. Optional: Stitch the darts in the tank front and the lining front (*fig. 1*).
2. Place the right side of the tank fabric to the right side of the lining fabric (both the front and the back) and stitch the armhole curves and the neckline (*fig. 2*). Trim the seams to 1/4" and clip the seam allowances (*fig. 3*).
3. Turn the fabric right side out and press the seams well (*fig. 4*).
4. Place the front and back with right sides together. Pin the shoulder seams of the tank fabric together going past the seam on both sides into the lining. Stitch as much of the seam as possible through the opening (*fig. 5*). Whip the remainder of the shoulder lining seam together by hand (*fig. 6*).
5. Flip the pieces, placing the tank front to the tank back and the tank front lining to the tank back lining. The armhole seam will match in the center. Stitch the side seams (*fig. 7*). Press seam open. Turn tank with right side out (*fig. 8*).
6. Hem the bottom of the tank by basting the tank fabric and the lining fabric together close to the bottom raw edge (*fig. 8*). Turn 1/8" to the wrong side then 1/4" and stitch in place (*fig. 9*).

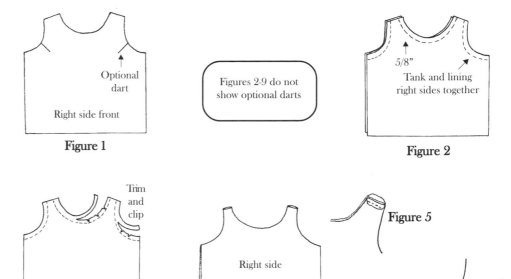

Optional dart

Right side front

Figure 1

Figures 2-9 do not show optional darts

5/8"

Tank and lining right sides together

Figure 2

Trim and clip

Figure 3

Right side

Figure 4

Figure 5

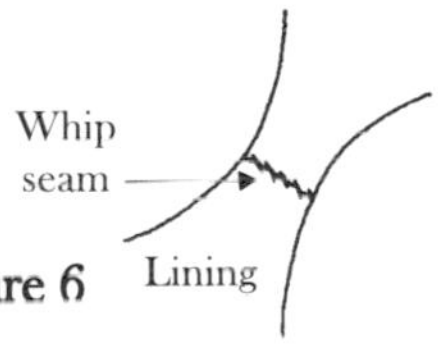

Whip seam

Lining

Figure 6

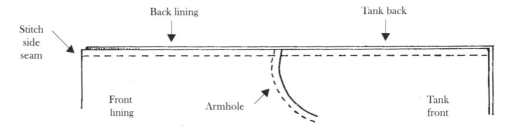

Back lining

Tank back

Stitch side seam

Front lining

Armhole

Tank front

Figure 7

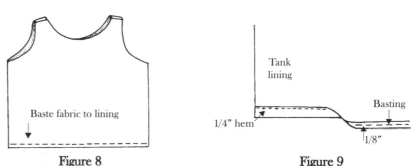

Baste fabric to lining

Figure 8

Tank lining

1/4" hem

Basting

1/8"

Figure 9

Shell - General Directions

Supplies

Note: An additional 3/8 yard of fabric is needed to cut the front and back facing for the V-neck shell. Please add this yardage to the yardage requirements below.

Long sleeve shell
- 45" fabric with or without nap
  XS - SM = 1-3/4 yards
  MD - LG = 2-1/2 yards
  XL - 2XL = 2-5/8 yards
  3XL = 2-7/8 yards
  4XL = 3-1/8 yards
- 60" fabric with or without nap
  XS = 1-5/8 yards
  SM - XL = 1-3/4 yards
  2XL - 4XL = 1-7/8 yards

Short sleeve shell
- 45" fabric
  XS - SM = 1-3/8 yards
  MD - LG = 2-1/8 yards
  XL - 2XL = 2-1/4 yards
  3XL = 2-1/2 yards
  4XL = 2-5/8 yards
- 60" fabric
  XS - LG = 1-3/8 yards
  XL = 1-1/2 yards
  2XL - 4XL = 1-7/8 yards
- One small button (1/2") for the Round Neck Version
- Thread to match fabric
- Basic sewing supplies

Pattern Pieces

- Shell Front with Dart or Shell Front (choose V-neck or round neck version)
- Shell Back
- Shell Short Sleeve or Shell Long Sleeve
- Front and Back Facings for V-neck Version

Cutting the Pieces

(refer to the layout)

- Cut a bias strip 2" wide by the neck measurement plus 1" for the bias neck facing if using the Round Neck Version – Bias Facing
- Cut a bias strip 1-3/4" wide by the neck measurement plus 1" for the bias neck binding if using the Round Neck Version – Bias Binding
- Cut one V-neck facing front on the fold if making the V-neck version
- Cut one V-neck facing back on the fold if making the V-neck version
- Cut a strip from the selvage 1" wide by 8" long for the back continous lap placket if using the round neck version
- Mark the darts if you chose the shell front with darts

* All seams are 5/8" unless otherwise noted. To finish seam, trim seam to 1/4" and overcast edge by machine or serger.

— Construction—

1. To make the placket in the back for the round neck version (Note: V-neck version does not have a placket):
   a. Cut a 4" slit down the center back from the neck edge (*fig. 1*).
   b. Place the selvage strip (1" x 8" placket piece) on top of the shell opening with raw edges even. The opening will be in a V- shape. Match the ends of the strip with the ends of the opening. Allow the point of the V to fall 1/8" below the cut edge of the strip. Pin in place. Stitch using a 1/8" seam (*fig. 2*).
   c. Fold the strip to the inside of the shell with the selvage edge just hiding the stitching line. Pin in place and stitch by hand or machine (*fig. 3*).
   d. Fold the placket in half and stitch a dart along the fold (*fig. 4*).
   e. Fold the left side of the placket to the inside of the blouse and leave the right side extended (*fig. 5*).

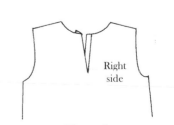

Figure 1

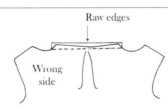

Raw edges

Wrong side

Figure 2

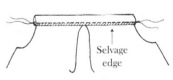

Selvage edge

Figure 3

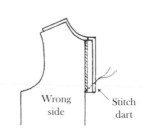

Wrong side

Stitch dart

Figure 4

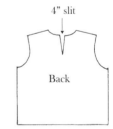

Right side

Figure 5

Shell - Round Neck Version

2. (Optional) Stitch the darts in the shell front *(fig. 6)*.

3. Place the front shell to the back shell at the shoulders, right sides together and stitch. Finish the seams *(fig. 7)*.

4. Finish the neck edge by one of the following three methods:

Round Neck Version – Bias Binding

a. Fold the 1-3/4" bias neck binding in half and press *(fig. 8)*.

b. Trim 5/8" from the neckline *(fig. 9)*, place the folded bias to the neck edge with the raw edges matching and leaving a portion of the binding extended on each end (this extended portion should be approximately 1/4"; trim extension if necessary) *(fig. 10)*.

c. Stitch the bias to the neck edge with a 1/4" seam. Clip seam allowance *(fig. 10)*.

d. Fold the extended ends flush with the edge of the shell *(fig. 11)*.

e. Flip the bias over the seam allowance and allow the fold of the bias to meet the stitching line on the wrong side of the shell. Stitch in place by hand or machine *(fig. 12)*.

Round Neck Version – Bias Facing

a. Fold the 2" bias neck facing in half and press *(fig. 13)*.

b. Place the folded bias to the neck edge with the raw edges matching and leaving a portion of the binding extended on each end (this extended portion should be approximately 1/4"; trim extension if necessary) *(fig. 14)*.

c. Stitch the facing to the neck edge with a 5/8" seam *(fig. 14)*. Trim seam to 1/4". Clip the seam allowance *(fig. 15)*.

d. Fold the extended ends flush with the back edge of the shell *(fig. 15)*.

e. Press the facing and seam allowance away from the neck opening. Understitch the facing through the trimmed seam *(fig. 16)*.

f. Turn the facing to the inside of the shell along the seam line. Stitch in place by hand or machine *(fig. 17)*.

Right side front

Stitch darts (Optional)

Figure 6

Wrong side front

Figure 7

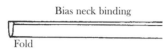

Bias neck binding

Fold

Figure 8

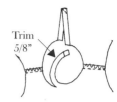

Trim 5/8"

Figure 9

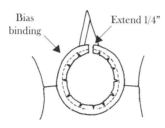

Bias binding

Extend 1/4"

Figure 10

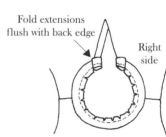

Fold extensions flush with back edge

Right side

Figure 11

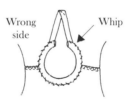

Wrong side

Whip

Figure 12

Bias neck facing

Fold and press

Figure 13

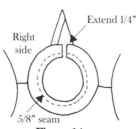

Extend 1/4"

Right side

5/8" seam

Figure 14

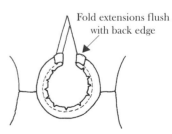

Fold extensions flush with back edge

Figure 15

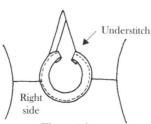

Understitch

Right side

Figure 16

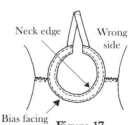

Neck edge

Wrong side

Bias facing

Figure 17

V-neck Version with Facing

a. Stitch the neck facing together at the shoulder seams *(fig. 18)*. Press the facing seams open and finish the outside edges of the facing with an overcast or serge *(fig. 19)*.

b. Fit the neck facing to the shell neck right sides together and pin in place. Stitch the neck facing to the neck line at 5/8" starting close to the shoulder seam *(fig. 20)*.

c. Trim and clip the seam *(fig. 20)*. Press the facing and seam allowance away from the garment. Understitch the facing through the facing and the trimmed seam *(fig. 21)*. Turn the facing to the inside of the shell and press well *(fig. 22)*.

5. Stitch two gathering rows in the top of the sleeves at 1/2" and 5/8" between the notches *(fig. 23)*. Place the sleeve to the arm opening, right sides together, matching the back shell to the sleeve back, front shell to sleeve front and the center of the sleeve to the shoulder seam. Ease the fullness of the sleeve to fit the arm opening. Stitch in place *(fig. 24)*. Finish the seam.

6. Place the sides and the sleeves of the shell, right sides together, and stitch. Finish the seams *(fig. 25)*.

7. Hem the Sleeves

   a. Short Sleeve: Hem the bottom of the sleeve by turning the edge of the sleeve to the inside 1/4" and then again 1-3/8" and stitch in place *(fig. 26)*.

   b. Long Sleeve: Hem the bottom of the sleeve by turning the edge of the sleeve to the inside 1/4" and then again 3/4" and stitch in place *(fig. 27)*.

8. Finish the bottom of the shell by turning the edge to the inside 1/4" and 1/2" again and top stitching in place *(fig. 27)*.

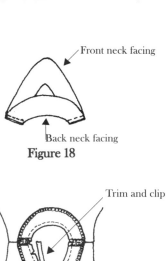

Front neck facing

Back neck facing

Figure 18

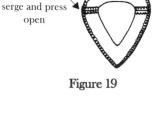

Overcast or serge and press open

Figure 19

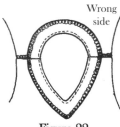

Trim and clip

Shell right side

Wrong side of facing

Figure 20

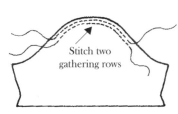

Understitch

Figure 21

Wrong side

Figure 22

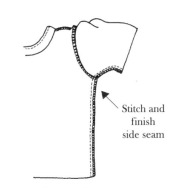

Stitch two gathering rows

Figure 23

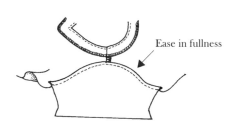

Ease in fullness

Figure 24

Stitch and finish side seam

Figure 25

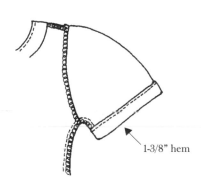

1-3/8" hem

Figure 26

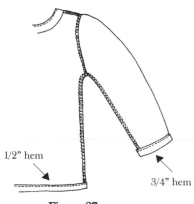

1/2" hem

3/4" hem

Figure 27

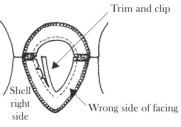

9. For Round Neck Versions only — Create a button loop on the left side of the back neck opening as follows:

a. Thread a hand needle with a double strand of thread and knot the end. At the top left hand side of the back opening, attach the thread to the inside edge of the fabric.

b. Bring the needle to the right side of the garment at A and take a small stitch (enter at B, exit at C) to create a loop in the thread, but do not pull the loop tight *(fig. 28)*. Holding the needle in the left hand, reach through the loop with the right index finger and pull a loop of the needle thread through the first loop *(fig. 29)*.

c. Pull on the second loop to tighten the first loop down close to the fabric a *(fig. 30)*. Use the right hand to pull new loop through *(fig. 31)* and tighten down the previous loop. Continue pulling loops through to create a chain stitch *(fig 32)*.

d. When the chain is long enough to make a loop that the button will pass through, pull the needle through the last loop and tighten it into a knot *(fig. 33)*.

e. Insert the needle through the fabric to the wrong side and tie off with a secure knot to complete the loop *(fig. 34)*.

10. For the Round Neck Versions only — Stitch a button opposite the loop at the neck edge.

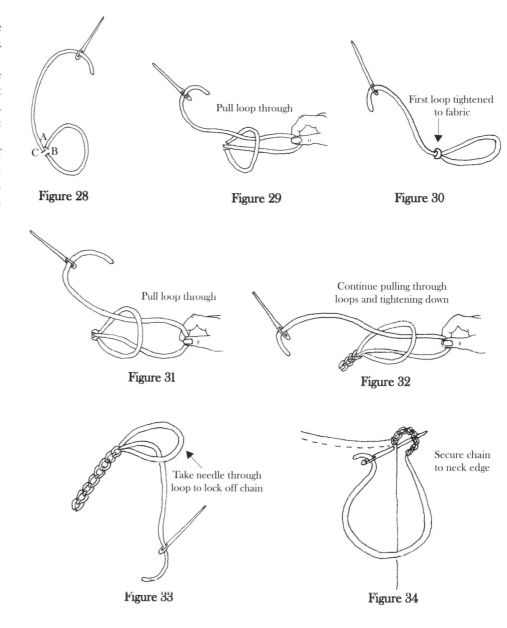

Figure 28

Pull loop through

Figure 29

First loop tightened to fabric

Figure 30

Pull loop through

Figure 31

Continue pulling through loops and tightening down

Figure 32

Take needle through loop to lock off chain

Figure 33

Secure chain to neck edge

Figure 34

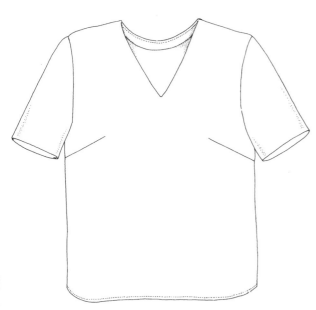

Shell - V Neck Version

Shell - Long Sleeve Version

Bias Skirt - General Directions

Supplies

- 60" Fabric with or without nap
  XS – SM = 2-3/8 yards
  MD = 2-1/2 yards
  LG = 2-5/8 yards
  XL = 2-3/4 yards
  2XL = 2-7/8 yards
  3XL = 3 yards
  4XL = 3-1/8 yards
- Thread to match fabric
- 1/4 yard of interfacing
- 1/2 yard of 1-1/4" wide elastic for sizes XS – LG or 3/4 yard of 1-1/4" wide elastic for size XL – 4XL
- Basic sewing supplies

Pattern Pieces

- Bias Skirt Front
- Bias Skirt Back
- Bias Skirt Front Waistband
- Bias Skirt Back Waistband

Cutting the Pieces

(refer to layout)

- Cut one full skirt front referring to the layout
- Cut one full skirt back referring to the layout
- Cut one skirt front waistband and one from interfacing
- Cut one skirt back waistband

* All seams are 5/8" unless otherwise noted. To finish seam, trim seam to 1/4" and overcast edge by machine or serger.

—Construction—

1. Stitch the skirt back waistband to the skirt back with right sides together. Finish the seam. Press the seam toward the waistband (*fig. 1*).
2. Finish the outer edge of the back waistband by turning 5/8" to the wrong side and press in place (*fig. 1*). Fold the waistband, matching the wrong sides and letting the folded edge of the band fall slightly below the seam line (*fig. 2*). Stitch the folded edge to the band at the seam line by stitching in the ditch on the right side (*fig. 3*).

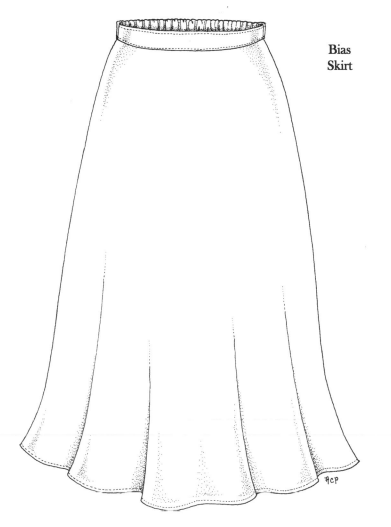

Bias Skirt

Waistband

Wrong side
skirt back

Figure 1

Wrong side

Figure 2

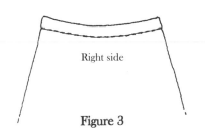

Right side

Figure 3

3. Run the elastic through the back waistband, stitching the elastic on one side and pinning on the other side *(fig. 4)*.

4. Attach the interfacing to the front waistband *(fig. 5)*.

5. With right sides together stitch the front waistband to the top of the skirt front. Press the seam toward the waistband *(fig. 6)*. Press under 5/8" along top edge of waistband.

6. Place the skirt front to the skirt back with right sides together matching the seam lines of the front and back waistbands. The front waistband will extend above the back waistband. On the side where you stitched the elastic, stitch the side and waistband seam. Finish the seam *(fig. 7)*.

7. On the side that you pinned the elastic, stitch the side seam up to the seam line attaching the band *(fig. 7)*. Try on the skirt and adjust the elastic to a comfortable fit. Pin the elastic at the edge of the band and trim away any excess elastic. Continue stitching the side seam of the waistband *(fig. 8)*.

8. Fold the front waistband to the wrong side over the back skirt elastic band. Stitch the waistband to the side seam *(fig. 9)*.

9. Flip the waistband to the front. Stitch the underside of the front waistband in place by stitching in the ditch from the right side *(fig. 10)*.

10. Hem the bottom of the skirt by serging or turning under 1/4" to the wrong side. Turn up again 3/8" and machine stitch the hem in place *(fig. 11)*.

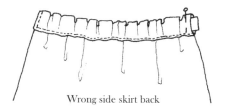

Wrong side skirt back

Figure 4

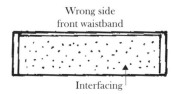

Wrong side front waistband

Interfacing

Figure 5

Wrong side skirt front

Figure 6

Wrong side skirt back

Figure 7

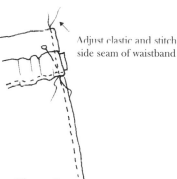

Adjust elastic and stitch side seam of waistband

Figure 8

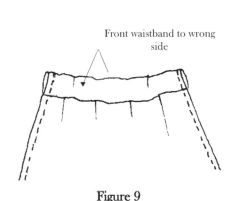

Front waistband to wrong side

Figure 9

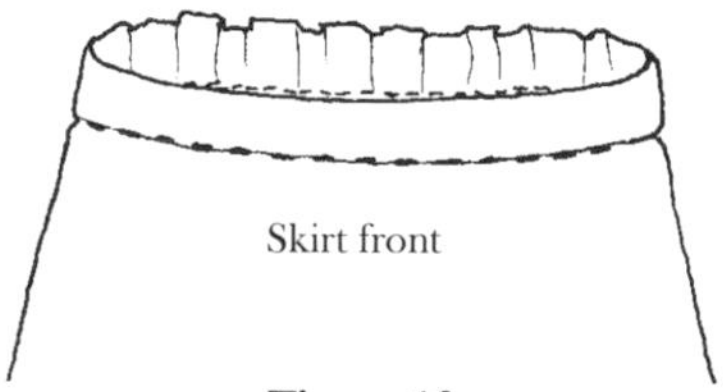

Skirt front

Figure 10

Stitch hem 3/8"

Figure 11

Gore Skirt - General Directions

Gore Skirt can be made with or without points.

Supplies

- 45" Fabric without nap
  XS = 4-1/4 yards
  SM – MD = 4-3/8 yards
  LG – XL = 4-1/2 yards
  2XL – 3XL = 4-7/8 yards
  4XL = 5 yards
- 45" Fabric with nap
  XS = 4-1/2 yards
  SM = 4-3/4 yards
  MD = 5 yards
  LG = 5-1/4 yards
  XL = 8-3/4 yards
  2XL – 4XL = 8-7/8 yards
- 60" Fabric with or without nap
  XS = 4-1/4 yards
  SM – MD = 4-3/8 yards
  LG – 4XL = 4-1/2 yards
- Thread to match fabric
- 2 yards of 1/2" wide elastic for sizes XS – LG and 3 yards of 1/2" wide elastic for sizes XL – 4XL
- Basic sewing supplies

Pattern Pieces

- Gore Skirt Panel

Cutting the pieces

(refer to layout)

- Cut eight skirt panels
- Cut two pieces of elastic the following measurement:
  XS – LG – Two 1 yard pieces
  XL – 4XL – Two 1-1/2 yard pieces

* All seams are 5/8" unless otherwise noted. To finish seam, trim seam to 1/4" and overcast edge by machine or serger.

—Construction—

1. With right sides together stitch the gores together with 5/8" seams to form a circle. Finish the seams (*fig. 1a or 1b*).
2. Serge or overcast the top edge of the skirt (*fig. 1a or 1b*).
3. Serge or overcast the bottom edge of the skirt (*fig. 1a or 1b*).
4. Turn down 1-1/2" in the top edge of the skirt to form a casing (*fig. 2*).
5. Stitch the casing in place near the edge of the overcast leaving 1" of the casing unstitched (*fig. 2*).

Gore Skirt without Points

**Figure 1a
Pointed Version**

**Figure 1b
Straight Version**

Leave open

1-1/2"

Figure 2

6. Measure from the top fold edge of the casing to the stitching near the edge of the overcast. Straight stitch in the center of this measurement around the skirt casing, leaving the same 1" unstitched *(fig. 3)*.
7. Thread the elastic through the two casings formed in the top of the skirt.
8. Thread both pieces at the same time. Pull the elastic through the casings *(fig. 4)*.
9. Try on the skirt and overlap the elastics to a comfortable fit. Stitch approximately 1" of the overlap and trim away any excess elastic from each end *(fig. 5)*.
10. Stretch the elastic so that the overlap slips into the casing. Stitch the 1" openings closed *(fig. 6)*.
11. Hem the bottom edge of the skirt by turning the serged or overcast edge to the wrong side 1/2" and straight stitch in place *(fig. 7a, pointed hem; fig. 7b, straight hem)*.

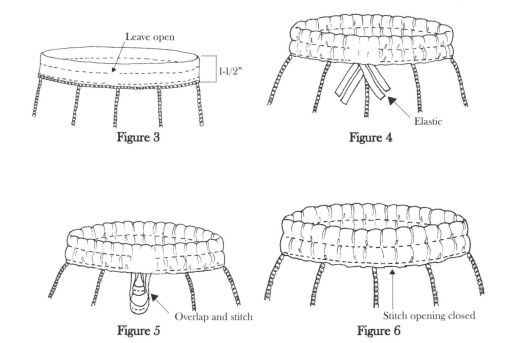

Leave open

1-1/2"

Figure 3

Elastic

Figure 4

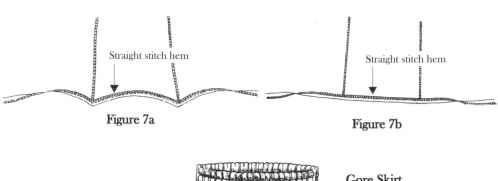

Overlap and stitch

Figure 5

Stitch opening closed

Figure 6

Straight stitch hem

Figure 7a

Straight stitch hem

Figure 7b

Gore Skirt with Points

Kimono Jacket - General Directions

Supplies

- 45" Fabric with or without nap
  SM - MD = 2-1/4 yards
  L – 4XL = N/A
- 60" fabric with or without nap
  XS – MD = 1-7/8 yards
  LG – XL = 2 yards
  2XL – 3XL = 2-1/4 yards
  4XL = 2-3/8 yards
- Thread to match fabric
- One yard interfacing
- Five buttons (5/8")
- Basic sewing supplies

Pattern Pieces

- Kimono Jacket Back
- Kimono Jacket Front
- Kimono Jacket Sleeve Band
- Kimono Jacket Front Facing
- Kimono Jacket Back Facing
- Kimono Jacket Front Band

Cutting the Pieces

(refer to layout)

- Cut one jacket back on the fold
- Cut two jacket fronts
- Cut two jacket sleeve bands – cut two from interfacing
- Cut two jacket front facings – cut two from interfacing
- Cut one jacket back facing on the fold – cut one on the fold from interfacing
- Cut two jacket front bands – cut two from interfacing

* All seams are 5/8" unless otherwise noted. To finish seam, trim seam to 1/4" and overcast edge by machine or serger.

—Construction—

1. With right sides together stitch the fronts to the back at the shoulder seams. Finish the seams *(fig.1)*.
2. Place the interfacing to the front and back neck facings and the front band. Baste the interfacing in place in the seam allowances *(fig. 2)*.
3. Stitch the front neck facings to the back neck facings at the shoulder seams *(fig. 3)*.
4. Place the neck facing to the neck of the jacket with right sides together. Stitch the facing to the jacket at the neck edge. Trim and clip the seam *(fig. 4)*. Press the neck facing to the wrong side of the jacket.

Kimono Jacket

Finish seam

Wrong side front

Figure 1

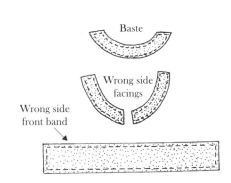

Baste

Wrong side facings

Wrong side front band

Figure 2

Figure 3

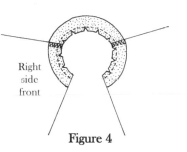

Right side front

Figure 4

5. Press under 1/4" on the outer edge of the jacket neck facing.

6. Pin facing in place. Stitch the facing in place stitching on the folded edge of the neck facing *(fig. 5)*.

7. With right sides together place the front to the back at the side and sleeve. Stitch the side and sleeve seam stopping at the dot on the bottom side seam. Clip through the seam allowance to the dot. Trim and finish the seam to the clip *(fig. 6)*.

8. Press up 1/4" on the bottom edge of the jacket. Press up a 3/4" hem on the bottom edge. Stitch the hem of the jacket on the folded edge *(fig. 7)*.

9. To finish the openings at the jacket sides, fold the seam allowance to each side and press *(fig. 8)*. Turn under 1/4" and press. Straight stitch from the hem up, across, and down to finish the opening *(fig. 9)*.

10. Stitch the front band to the jacket front with right sides together, leaving the fabric extended 5/8" above the edge of the neck and 5/8" below the bottom edge of the jacket *(fig. 10)*. Press the seam and the band away from the jacket *(fig. 11)*.

11. Fold the band to the outside with right sides together on the fold line *(fig. 12)*. The raw edge of the band will extend past the seam line. Stitch the band together at the top and bottom edges, following the finished edges of the jacket. Trim the seam *(fig. 13)*.

12. Flip the band to the inside. Press the top and bottom seams. Turn under the outer edge of the band to just cover the band seam *(fig. 14)*.

13. Stitch the backside of the band in place by stitching in the front band seam *(fig. 15)*.

14. Mark buttonholes and stitch. Mark button placement and sew on buttons *(fig. 16)*.

15. Stitch the side of the sleeve band with right sides together *(fig. 17)*. Press the seam open.

16. Fold the sleeve band with wrong sides together and press *(fig. 18)*.

17. Fit the sleeve band to the bottom of the sleeve with right sides together and stitch in place *(fig. 19)*. Finish the seam. Press the band in place away from the sleeve *(fig. 20)*.

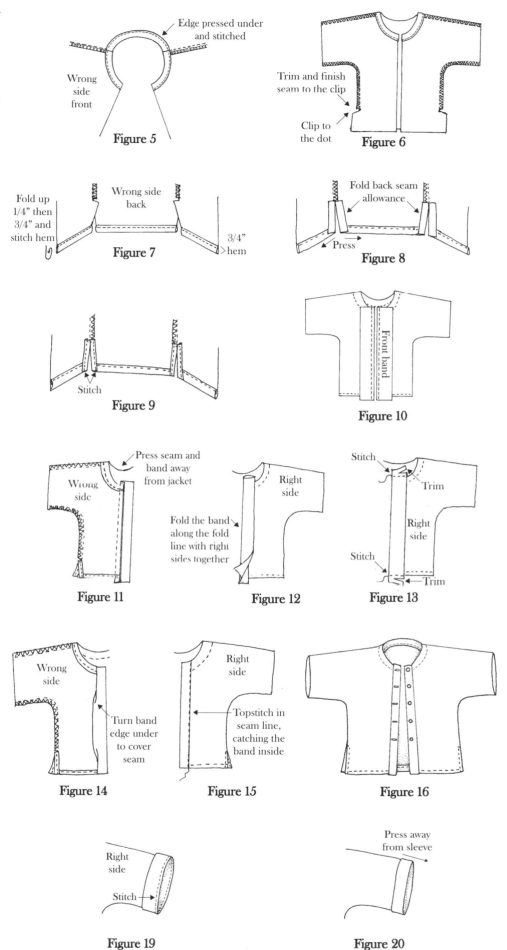

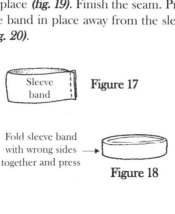

Long Sleeve Jacket - General Directions

Supplies

- 45" Fabric with or without nap
  XS – MD = 2-7/8 yards
  LG = 3-1/4 yards
  XL – 2XL = 3-3/8 yards
  3XL – 4XL = 3-3/4 yards
- 60" Fabric with or without nap
  XS – MD = 2-1/4 yards
  LG – XL = 2-3/8 yards
  2XL – 3XL = 2-3/4 yards
  4XL = 2-7/8 yards
- Thread to match fabric
- XS – MD = 1-3/8 yards interfacing
- LG – 4XL = 1-3/4 yards interfacing
- 7 buttons (5/8")
- Basic sewing supplies

Pattern Pieces

- Long Sleeve Jacket Front
- Long Sleeve Jacket Back
- Long Sleeve Jacket Sleeve
- Long Sleeve Jacket Pocket
- Long Sleeve Jacket Front Band and Facing
- Long Sleeve Jacket Back Facing
- Long Sleeve Jacket Sleeve Facing Cuff

Cutting the Pieces

(refer to layout)

- Cut two jacket fronts
- Cut one jacket back on the fold
- Cut two jacket sleeves
- Cut four jacket pockets
- Cut two jacket front band and facing and two from interfacing
- Cut one jacket back facing on the fold and one from interfacing
- Cut two jacket sleeve facing cuffs and two from interfacing

* All seams are 5/8" unless otherwise noted. To finish seam, trim seam to 1/4" and overcast edge by machine or serger.

—Construction—

1. Mark darts in the jacket front. Stitch darts. Press in place *(fig. 1)*.
2. With right sides together stitch the fronts to the back at the shoulder seams. Press the seams open *(fig. 2)*.
3. Place the interfacing to the front facings and the back facing. Baste the interfacing in place along the seam allowances *(fig. 3)*.
4. Stitch the back neck facing to the front facings at the shoulder seams with right sides together *(fig. 4)*. Press the seams open.
5. Place the front facings to the fronts with right sides together and stitch in place along the front edges *(fig. 5)*. Press the seam toward the facing.

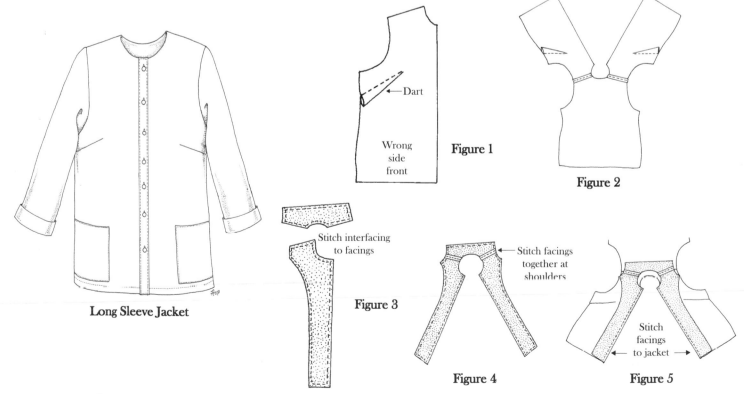

Long Sleeve Jacket

Dart

Wrong side front

Figure 1

Figure 2

Stitch interfacing to facings

Figure 3

Stitch facings together at shoulders

Figure 4

Stitch facings to jacket

Figure 5

6. Fold the right side of the facing to the right sides of the jacket along the fold line matching the shoulder seams and the neck edges. Stitch the neck edge seam *(fig. 6)*. Trim and clip the seam. Turn the facing to the wrong side. Understitch the neck facing *(fig. 7)*, stitching only through the seam allowance and the facing.

7. Finish the edges of the facing on the front and back with a serger or by turning under 1/8" and stitching in place *(see fig. 7)*. The shoulder edge of the facing will be finished after inserting the sleeve.

8. Press the facing in place around the neck and along the fold line of the front facing. This will form a placket along the front of the jacket *(fig. 8)*. Note that the facing wraps to the jacket front, forming a front placket. Secure the facing in place at the seam line for the sleeve by basting in the seam allowance *(fig. 9)*.

9. Fit the sleeve to the armhole with right sides together and stitch in place. Finish the seam *(fig. 10)*. Stitch an ease line between the dots as indicated on the sleeve pattern. This will give a slight fullness at the elbow.

10. Place the pockets and the pocket lining with right sides together. Stitch the top, one side and the bottom of the pockets together with a 5/8" seam *(fig. 11)*. Leave one pocket open on the left side, and one pocket open on the right side. Trim, turn right side out and press.

11. Topstitch close to the top edge of each pocket to hold the lining in place *(fig. 12)*.

12. Place the pocket on the jacket front matching the notches.

13. Stitch the pocket in place close to the folded edge on the side and the bottom. Pin or baste the raw edge of the pocket to the side of the jacket front *(fig. 13)*.

14. With right sides together matching the edge of the sleeve, the underarm seam and the bottom of the jacket, stitch the sleeve and side seams of the jacket easing in the fullness on the sleeve seam *(fig. 14)*. Finish the seam.

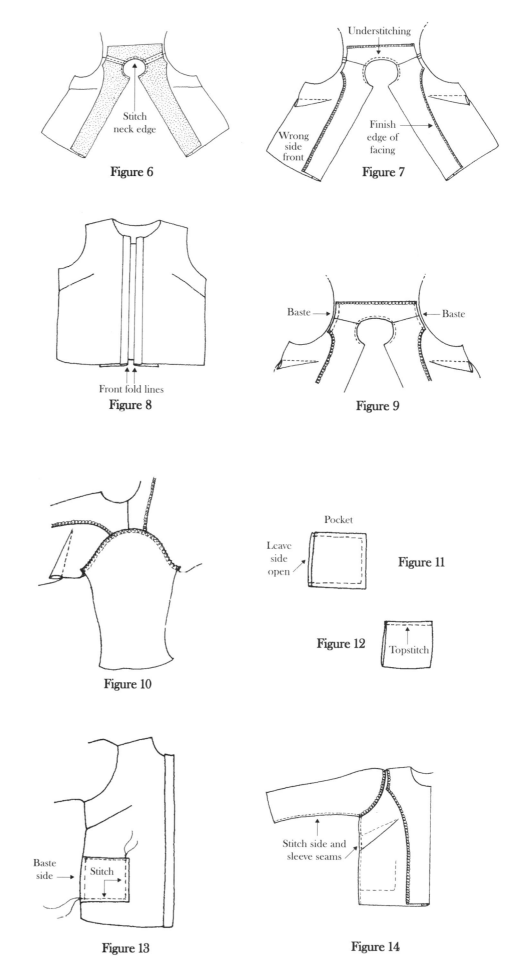

Figure 6

Figure 7

Figure 8

Figure 9

Figure 10

Figure 11

Figure 12

Figure 13

Figure 14

15. Turn the facing at the bottom front edge to the right side on the facing fold line. Stitch the facing in place 7/8" from the edge *(fig. 15)*. Turn the facing to the wrong side and press *(fig. 16)*.

16. To form the hem in the jacket, press under to the wrong side 3/8" along the bottom of the jacket. Turn up to the wrong sides again 1/2". Stitch in place around the bottom of the jacket, stitching on the top folded edge, starting and stopping at the facing edge on each side *(fig. 17)*.

17. Stitch the front facing in place by stitching in the seam line from the neckline to the bottom of the jacket *(fig. 18)*.

18. Place the sleeve facing /cuff interfacings to the wrong side of the sleeve facing/cuffs. Baste the interfacing in place in the seam allowances *(fig. 19)*.

19. With right sides together stitch the side of the cuff facings together *(fig. 20)*. Clip the seam and press the seam open.

20. With right sides together fit the cuff to the bottom of the sleeve and stitch *(fig. 21)*. Trim the seam and press the sleeve facing/cuff away from the sleeve. Finish the edge of the cuff with an overcast or serger *(fig. 22)* or turn under 1/4" and press in place. Fold the cuff to the inside and stitch in place on the folded or serged edge *(fig. 23)*.

21. Mark buttonholes on the right front placket and stitch buttonholes.

22. Mark placement for buttons on the left front placket and sew on buttons.

23. Turn the cuff up on the fold line *(fig. 24)*.

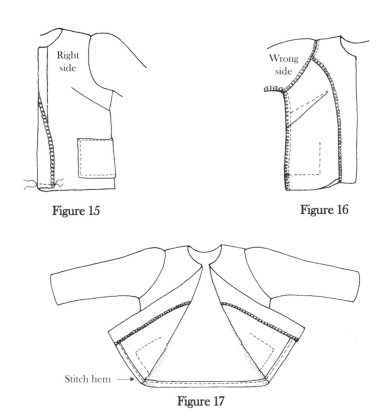

Figure 15

Figure 16

Figure 17

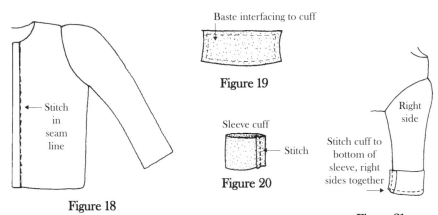

Figure 18

Figure 19

Figure 20

Figure 21

Figure 22

Figure 23

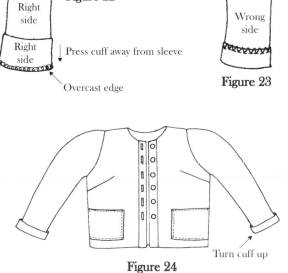

Figure 24

Rust Jacket with Ultrasuede™

Made of rust rayon fabric, this long sleeve jacket was made for Martha Pullen. The jacket features tan Ultrasuede™ shaped in a "V" on the front, down both sides of the front, on the pockets, and on the cuffs of the sleeves. Rust beads are stitched underneath the Ultrasuede™ strips which run diagonally on the jacket. Beautiful decorative buttons are used to close the front of the suit. The bias skirt, made of rust rayon fabric, finishes the look of this suit that is flattering on so many figure types.

- This jacket was made with reference to the Long Sleeve Jacket General Directions found on page 16.

- The skirt was made by the Bias Skirt General Directions found on page 10.

Supplies

- Refer to the yardage for the Long Sleeve Jacket, adding 1/2 yard to the total for the overlay
- 1/4 yard of Ultrasuede™ for trim
- 1 yard of beaded trim
- Decorative thread to match ultra suede
- Sewing thread to match the fabric
- Basic sewing supplies

Pattern Pieces

- Refer to the pattern pieces needed for the Long Sleeve Jacket General Directions
- Jacket front overlay template created per instructions

Cutting the Pieces

(Refer to the layout for Long Sleeve Jacket)
- Cut four Ultrasuede™ strips 1-1/8 by 45"
- Cut two overlays from the template created below
- Refer to the Long Sleeve Jacket General Directions, Cutting the Pieces and cut the pieces listed

*   All seams are 5/8" unless otherwise noted. To finish seam, trim seam to 1/4" and overcast edge by machine or serger.

Creating an Overlay Template for the Jacket Front

1. Trace the upper half of the Long Sleeve Jacket Front onto tissue paper.
2. From the sleeve edge of the shoulder seam measure in 1-7/8" and place a dot (**fig. 1**).
3. Measure from the neck edge down 8" along the front edge of the tissue paper (**fig. 1**).
4. Draw a line connecting the two dots (**fig. 1**).
5. Cut along the drawn line and discard the lower portion of the tissue paper. Mark the upper portion "Overlay for Jacket Front."

Rust Jacket with Ultrasuede™

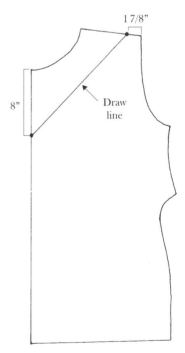

Figure 1

—Directions—

1. Finish the edge of the jacket overlay by placing the right side of the ultrasuede to the wrong side of the jacket overlay fabric and stitch with a 5/8" seam. Trim the seam to 1/8" *(fig. 2)*. Press the Ultrasuede™ to the right side.

2. Stitch the Ultrasuede™ in place with a pinstitch or blanket stitch *(fig. 3)*.

3. Attach the beading by hand to the underside of the finished edge of the overlay. Trim away beads that would interfere with jacket construction *(fig. 4)*.

4. Place the overlays on the jacket fronts and baste in place.

5. Pin a strip of Ultrasuede™ to the jacket fronts with the wrong side of Ultrasuede™ to the right side of the jacket. Stitch the Ultrasuede™ to the jacket with a pinstitch or blanket stitch *(fig. 5)*.

6. Pin a strip of Ultrasuede™ to the top of each of the pockets. Stitch the Ultrasuede™ to the pocket with a pinstitch or blanket stitch *(fig. 6)*.

7. Pin a strip of Ultrasuede™ to the top of two of the sleeve cuffs. Stitch the Ultrasuede™ in place with a pinstitch or blanket stitch *(fig. 7)*. Treat the Ultrasuede™ and pocket as one piece.

8. Refer to the Long Sleeve Jacket General Directions, steps 1 – 22 to complete the jacket. The cuff is left extended, not folded up.

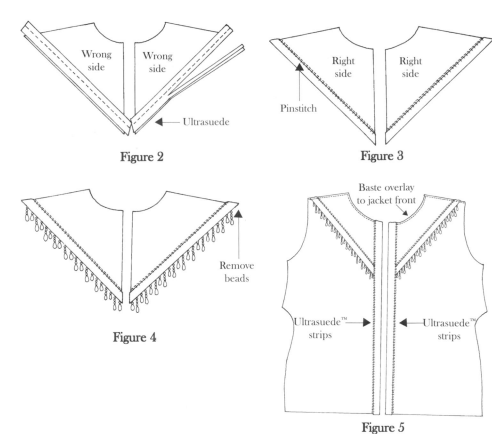

Figure 2

Figure 3

Figure 4

Figure 5

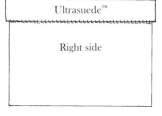

Figure 6

Figure 7

Detail of Rust Jacket with Ultrasuede™

Rust Tank

Made of rust rayon fabric, this sleeveless tank top is embellished with loops of tan bias Ultrasuede, stitched down with a pinstitch. This particular tank is lined.

- This tank was made with reference to the Tank General Directions – Lined Version found on page 5.

Supplies

- For fabric requirements, see Tank General Directions
- 1/8 yard of Ultrasuede™ for trim
- Decorative thread to match Ultrasuede™
- Sewing thread to match the fabric
- Basic sewing supplies

* All seams are stitched 5/8" and trimmed to 1/4" unless otherwise noted.

Pattern Pieces

- Tank Front
- Tank Back
- Rust Tank Template

Cutting the Pieces
(refer to the layout)

- Cut one tank front on the fold and one tank back on the fold from the tank fabric
- Cut one tank front on the fold and one tank back on the fold from the lining fabric
- Cut two strips of ultra suede 3/8" wide by 45"
- Optional: Mark the darts in the tank front

—Directions—

1. Trace the template onto the center front of the tank and shape the Ultrasuede™ strips (centering along the template lines). Pin in place *(fig. 1)*.
2. Pinstitch or blanket stitch the edge of the Ultrasuede™ trim to the tank front *(fig. 2)*.
3. Refer to the Tank-Lined Version General Directions, steps 1 - 6 and complete the lined tank.

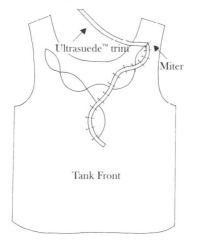

Figure 1

Figure 2

Rust Tank

Detail of Rust Tank

Instant Appliqué/Stippled Kimono Jacket

Made of white linen with purple stippling all over the jacket, this is a very interesting garment with a creative instant appliqué technique. For the instant appliqué, use any outline machine embroidery design; this one was originally for redwork. You can put together 4X4 designs to make the larger design as shown here if you do not have a large embroidery hoop. After outlining the flowers and leaves in the red and green, use colored pencils to color in the inside; fabric markers are another option. This type of technique is very quick and easy and totally unique. The birds are made using the same technique.

The white jacket is machine stippled in purple thread with garment-weight batting underneath. A narrow white linen binding finishes the sleeves. The front plackets are also of white linen. This jacket is so cute when worn with the pretty lined tank and bias skirt in a lavender print with yellow and green. Eileen Roche with Amazing Designs made this wonderfully fun outfit.

- This jacket was made with reference to the Kimono Jacket General Directions found on page 14.
- The skirt was made by the Bias Skirt General Directions found on page 10.
- The tank was made by the Tank General Directions - Lined Version found on page 5.
- The jacket embroidery is from Very Versatile Redwork by Eileen Roche (AD3007) available from Amazing Designs or you may choose another outline type embroidery.

Supplies

- Refer to the fabric yardage in the Kimono Jacket General Directions (buttons are optional)
- Fabric for lining jacket – purchase same amount as for jacket
- Colored pencils or markers: Prismacolor® colored pencils were used (will fade after washing) or you can use Marvy® fabric markers
- Contrasting threads for embroidery design and for stippling
- Garment-weight batting for quilting the jacket (same yardage as for jacket)
- Medium sized safety pins
- Tear-away stabilizer
- Basic sewing supplies

Pattern Pieces

- Refer to the pattern pieces needed for the Kimono Jacket General Directions
- Alter Kimono Jacket pattern pieces – shorten the jacket front, jacket back and jacket front band 6-1/2"
- Alter Kimono Jacket Sleeve Band - fold the pattern along the fold line creating a pattern piece 2-1/2" wide by the length for each size

Cutting the Pieces

- Cut a rectangle of fabric 1" larger on all four sides than the shortened jacket back pattern (remember that the back is on the fold so you will need a rectangle twice as wide as the jacket back pattern piece). Cut one lining rectangle the same size. Cut one batting rectangle the same size.
- Cut two rectangles of fabric 1" larger on all four sides than the shortened jacket front pattern. Cut two lining rectangles the same size. Cut two batting rectangles the same size.
- Cut two shortened Kimono Jacket Front Bands
- Cut two Sleeve Bands by the altered pattern
- Cut one Kimono Jacket Back Facing on the fold
- Cut two Kimono Jacket Front Facings

Jacket Front

Jacket Back

—Directions—

1. Trace the jacket back outline onto the fabric rectangle for the jacket back. Choose an embroidery outline design and stitch in approximately the positions shown in *figure 1*, using tear-away stabilizer beneath the fabric.

2. When stitching is complete, remove the stabilizer.

3. Use the colored pencils or fabric markers to shade and color the inside of the design. Set the colors according to the pen directions, or heat-set colored pencils by pressing with a press cloth.

4. Layer the back lining rectangle (wrong side up), the back batting rectangle and the jacket back rectangle (right side up). Pin the layers together with the safety pins *(fig. 2)*.

5. Refer to the technique Stipple Stitching and stitch a loose stipple pattern approximately 1" beyond the drawn outline of the jacket back. Do not stipple over the embroidery design—stipple around it *(fig. 3)*. Remove the pins as you stipple.

6. Repeat steps 1-5 for the two jacket front rectangles. Be sure to trace a left and right front *(fig. 4)*.

7. Re-trace the jacket back and jacket front patterns onto the embroidered and stippled rectangles in case the stippling has "shrunk" the rectangles.

8. Cut the back and two fronts along the lines re-traced in step 7 *(fig. 5)*.

9. Refer to the directions for the Kimono Jacket, steps 1-4 and complete the steps. Understitch the neck facing. Finish the outer edge of the neck facing by overcasting the outer edge.

10. Fold the sleeve bands in half lengthwise with wrong sides together and press *(fig. 6)*.

11. Pin the raw edges of the folded sleeve bands to the lower edge of each sleeve and stitch with a 1/2" seam *(fig. 7)*. Press the sleeve band and seam allowance away from the sleeve *(fig. 8)*.

12. Place the jacket fronts and back right sides together and stitch the side seams from the lower edge of the jacket to the edge of the sleeve band. Finish the seam *(fig. 9)*.

13. Serge or overcast the lower edge of the jacket *(fig. 9)*.

14. Turn the lower edge of the jacket to the wrong side 1/2" and hand whip or machine stitch the hem in place *(fig. 10)*.

15. Refer to the directions for the Kimono Jacket, steps 10-13 and complete the steps.

16. Fold the sleeve bands to the wrong side to cover the seam and to fall just above the seam line. Stitch the edge in place by stitching in the ditch *(fig. 11)*.

17. Buttons and buttonholes may be added if desired.

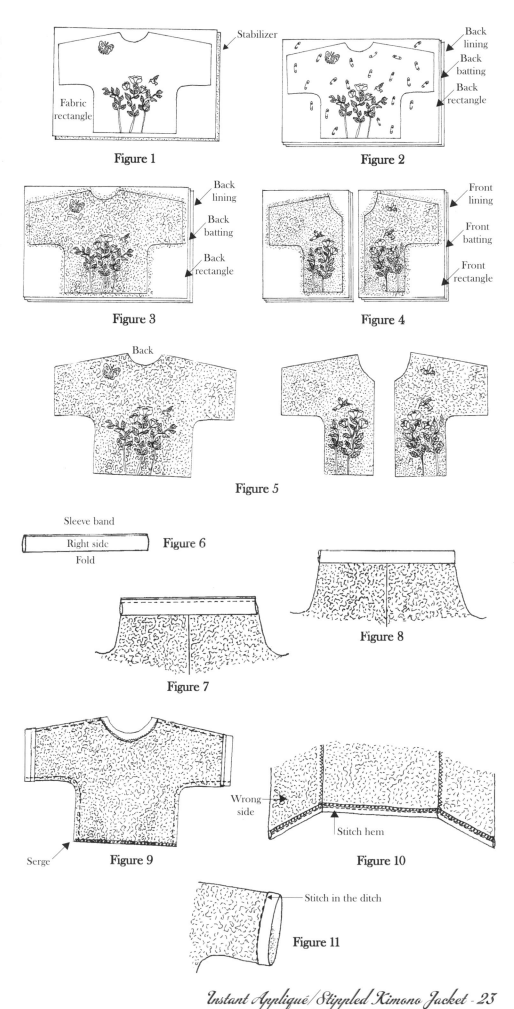

Figure 1

Figure 2

Figure 3

Figure 4

Figure 5

Figure 6

Figure 7

Figure 8

Figure 9

Figure 10

Figure 11

Instant Appliqué/Stippled Kimono Jacket - 23

Circular Embroidered Jacket

Linnette Whicker, a Pfaff educator, created this fantasy of elegance made of off-white handkerchief linen and magnificent machine embroidery. Using a circular attachment, different sized half circles are stitched on the pockets, the sleeves, the blouse and the skirt; the stitch is wing-needle entredeux. The back of the jacket has a complete circle of the wing-needle entredeux with a beautiful large peach and green embroidered flower design. The sleeves of the jacket have half circles of the wing-needle entredeux with decorative stitches inside each half circle. The circular attachment is used for both the half circles as well as the decorative stitches within the half circles. All of the entredeux stitching is done in ccru thread. The front of the jacket closes with self-covered buttons and buttonholes.

- This jacket was made with reference to the Long Sleeve Jacket General Directions found on page 16.

Note: This jacket was embroidered using a Pfaff 2140. The embroidery on the back of the jacket is from Card #300, design #11. The circle on the jacket back and the partial circles were sewn with stitch #142 (W=3.5, L=3.0) using a wing needle. Decorative stitches were used inside the partial circles on the pockets and sleeves. The Pfaff circular guide was used for the partial circles on the pockets and sleeves.

Supplies

- Refer to the Long Sleeve Jacket General Directions for the fabric and notions requirements; use six self-covered buttons, 7/8"
- Tear-away stabilizer
- Alcazar™ rayon thread in the following colors: Cream, #556; Peach, #701; Green, #719; OR Sulky® thread may be substituted in the following colors: Cream, #1022; Med. Peach, #1015; Mint Green, #1047
- #12/80 universal needle
- #100 wing or #120 universal needle
- Thread to match fabric
- Circular guide or use templates provided
- Basic sewing supplies

Pattern Pieces

- Refer to the pattern pieces listed in the Long Sleeve Jacket General Directions
- Circle Template for Jacket Back or use the circular guide with your machine
- Half Circle Template for Jacket Sleeve and Pocket or use the circular guide with your machine

Cutting the Pieces

- Refer to the layout guide for the Long Sleeve Jacket

* All seams are 5/8" unless otherwise noted. To finish seam, trim seam to 1/4" and overcast edge by machine or serger.

—Directions—

1. Place tear-away stabilizer beneath the fabric before completing the embroidery.
2. Embellish the jacket back with the embroidery design from Card #300, design 11 or another design of your choice. If choosing another embroidery, it should fit within the circle template for the jacket back. The center of the design is 7" down from the neck edge at the center of the jacket and the circle has a diameter of 8-1/4". It is suggested that the embroidery be done first and then encircled with the wing needle and an entredeux stitch (W=3.5, L=3.0) *(fig. 1)*.

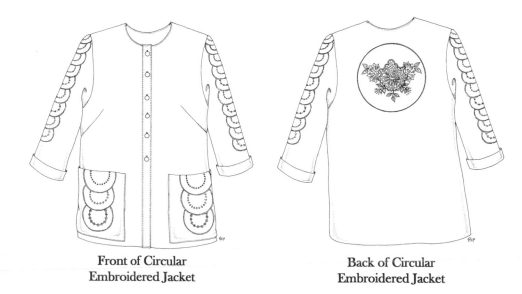

Front of Circular Embroidered Jacket

Back of Circular Embroidered Jacket

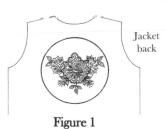

Jacket back

Figure 1

3. Embellish the jacket sleeves and pockets in the center with partial circles using an entredeux stitch (W=3.5, L=3.0) with the circular guide and wing needle. The circular guide must be repositioned to stitch decorative stitches within each circle *(fig. 2)*. If a circular guide is not available, use the sleeve template provided.

4. Remove the tear-away stabilizer from behind the fabric before beginning construction.

5. Refer to the Long Sleeve Jacket General Directions, steps 1 – 23 and complete the steps.

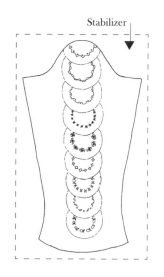

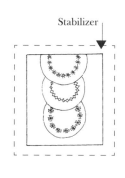

Figure 2

Circular Embroidered Shell

This short sleeve shell features more half circles stitched in wing-needle baby daisy entredeux. A beautiful flower design is found on the front of the shell in peach and green threads. The sleeves are hemmed with baby daisy wing-needle entredeux, with the same entredeux in half circles all the way around the sleeves.

This shell was made with reference to the Shell General Directions found on page 6.

Note: This shell was embroidered using a Pfaff 2140. The embroidery is from Flower Card #309, design #6. The half circles were sewn with stitch #159 (W=3.5, L=5.0) using a circular guide with the machine.

Supplies

- Refer to the Shell General Directions, Short Sleeve Version for the fabric requirements
- Tear-away stabilizer
- Alcazar™ rayon thread in the following colors: Cream, #556; Peach, #701; Green, #719 or Sulky® thread may be substituted in the following colors: Cream, #1022; Med. Peach, #1015; Mint Green, #1047
- #12/80 universal needle
- #100 wing or #120 universal needle
- One small button (1/2")
- Thread to match fabric
- Circular guide for machine (optional)
- Basic sewing supplies

Pattern Pieces

- Shell Front without dart—Round Neck Version
- Shell Back
- Shell Short Sleeve
- Half Circle Template for Shell Front
- Half Circle Template for Shell Sleeve

Cutting the Pieces

- Cut a rectangle large enough to fit the shell front onto. Trace the shell front cutting lines onto the rectangle.
- Cut the remaining pieces, referring to the General Directions and Shell layout
- Cut a bias strip 2" wide by the neck measurement plus 1"
- Cut a strip from the selvage 1" wide by 8" long

* All seams are 5/8" unless otherwise noted. To finish seam, trim seam to 1/4" and overcast edge by machine or serger.

Circular Embroidered Shell

—Directions—

1. Choose the embroidery listed above or choose another embroidery measuring approximately 1-5/8" by 9". Using tear-away stabilizer, stitch the embroidery down the center front beginning 1-5/8" from the drawn edge of the neck *(fig. 1)*. Remove the stabilizer and press the piece well.

2. Center the Half Circle Template 1" below the end of center embroidery and trace straight lines. If you do not have a circular guide with your machine, trace the half circles from the template also.

3. Stitch the half circles around the rectangle using an entredeux stitch or a daisy type stitch on your machine. Stabilizer may be needed behind the fabric.

4. Stitch the straight lines of the rectangle *(fig. 2)*. Remove all stabilizer. Press the piece well.

5. Cut out the shell front along the drawn cutting lines.

6. Draw a line 2-7/8" from the bottom cut edge of each sleeve. Place the Half Circle Template for Shell Sleeve onto the drawn line, centering one of the half circles at the center of the sleeve. Move the template until a complete pattern has been drawn on the sleeves. You may use the circle guide for completing the half circles if one is available *(fig. 3)*.

7. Place stabilizer beneath the fabric. Stitch the half circles on each sleeve using a decorative stitch and a wing needle *(fig. 3)*. The straight line of decorative stitching will be done after the shell is constructed *(see fig. 4)*.

8. Refer to the Shell General Directions, steps 1, 3, 4, Round Neck Version – Bias Facing, 5 and 6.

9. Fold a 1-5/8" hem to the wrong side of each sleeve. With stabilizer under the layers, stitch along the straight line drawn in step 6. The stitching should catch the hem of the sleeve *(fig. 4)*. Remove the stabilizer. On the inside of the sleeve, trim away any excess fabric above the decorative stitching *(fig. 5)*.

10. Refer to the Shell General Directions, steps 8, 9 and 10 to complete the shell.

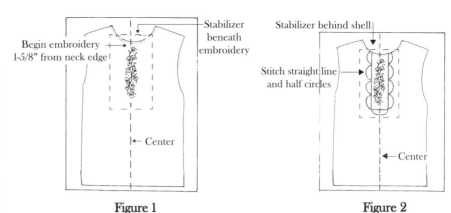

Figure 1

Begin embroidery 1-5/8" from neck edge

Stabilizer beneath embroidery

Center

Stabilizer behind shell

Stitch straight line and half circles

Center

Figure 2

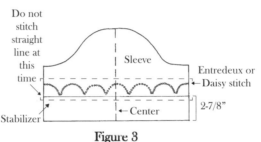

Do not stitch straight line at this time

Sleeve

Entredeux or Daisy stitch

2-7/8"

Stabilizer

Center

Figure 3

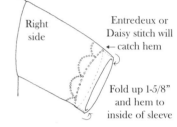

Right side

Entredeux or Daisy stitch will catch hem

Fold up 1-5/8" and hem to inside of sleeve

Figure 4

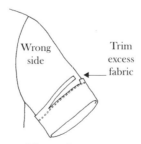

Wrong side

Trim excess fabric

Figure 5

Circular Embroidered Skirt

This bias skirt features half-circle wing needle entredeux shapes meeting halfway along a straight seam of the wing needle entredeux. The half circles go all the way around the skirt. Inside the half circles on the front of the skirt are little peach and green machine-embroidered heart designs with leaves.

- This skirt was made with reference to the Bias Skirt General Directions found on page 10.

Note: This skirt was embroidered using a Pfaff 2140. The embroidery inside the partial circles is from the Pfaff Martha Pullen card #1004, designs #9 and #10. The partial circles were sewn with stitch #142 (W=3.5, L=3.0) using a wing needle. The Pfaff circular guide was used for the partial circles on the skirt.

Supplies

- Refer to the Bias Skirt General Directions for the fabric requirements
- Tear-away stabilizer
- Alcazar™ rayon thread in the following colors: Cream, #556; Peach, #701; Green, #719 or other decorative thread may be substituted in the following colors: Cream, #1022; Mcd. Peach, #1015; Mint Green, #1047

- #11/80 universal needle
- #100 wing or #120 universal needle
- Thread to match fabric
- Circular guide for machine (optional)
- Thread to match fabric
- 1/4 yard of interfacing
- 1/2 yard of 1-1/4" wide elastic for sizes XS – LG and 3/4 yard of 1-1/4" wide elastic for sized XL – 4XL
- Basic sewing supplies

Pattern Pieces

- Refer to the pieces listed in the Bias Skirt General Directions
- Skirt Template

Cutting the Pieces

- Refer to the layout for the bias skirt

* All seams are .5/8" unless otherwise noted. To finish seam, trim seam to 1/4" and overcast edge by machine or serger.

Directions

1. Refer to the Bias Skirt General Directions and complete steps 1 – 9.
2. Draw a line for the center of the design 5" from the bottom of the hem with a wash-out marker.
3. Trace the skirt template onto the lower edge of the skirt matching the line 5" from the bottom of the hem. Continue tracing the template around the skirt. Adjust the template so that the circles meet the beginning of the template.
4. With stabilizer under the fabric, stitch along the drawn lines using an entredeux stitch. If a circular guide is available, refer to the circular guide directions from your sewing machine company.
5. Embroider the designs in the half circles in the front of the skirt using the embroidery listed above or an embroidery of your choice (see finished drawing). Remove all stabilizer and press well.
6. Refer to the Bias Skirt General Directions and complete step 10.

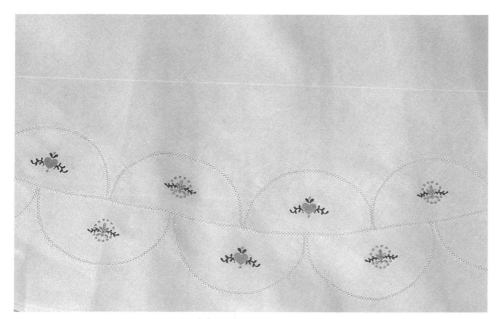

Detail of Circular Embroidered Skirt

Purchased Linen Towel Suit

When I saw these bath-sized, linen imported towels, I thought, "I just have to have a suit made with these." Sue Pennington heard my plea and told me she thought the best suit pattern in this book would be the long-sleeved jacket with the tank for a blouse; Sue knows that I usually wear sleeveless shells underneath my suits. She used seven of the bath--sized imported towels to create this suit. The towels come in white; I don't usually wear white, so Sue dyed the garment ecru with Rit® dye in the washing machine. The massive embroidered embellishment on the towels makes further embellishment unnecessary. The front of the jacket is closed with beautiful pearl buttons with a gold band around each button.

Ecru linen blend is used for the tank top. The tank top has a beautiful large embroidery on the upper front; the bias binding around the neckline and the armholes is stitched down with wing needle entredeux. Since the skirt is also made of towels, we are giving you directions for a straight skirt, which has side slits and elastic all the way around the waistline.

- This jacket was made with reference to the Long Sleeve Jacket General Directions found on page 16.

- The tank was made by the Tank General Directions, Unlined Version found on page 3. The embroidery listed below was added below the neckline on the front of the tank.

- The tank embroidery is Husqvarna Viking Embroidery Card #25, Design #21. Place one full design in the center and 1/2 design on each side tilting the design to curve with the neckline.

* All seams are 5/8" unless otherwise noted. To finish the seams, trim to 1/4" and overcast the edges by machine or serger.

Supplies

- 5 linen bath towels for jacket and 2 for the skirt (28" by 41") Five towels will make up to a size XL jacket. For larger sizes you would need a wider linen or purchase an additional towel for the back side additions. An additional towel may be needed for the larger size skirt.
- 1-1/4 yards of 3/4" elastic for the skirt
- RIT® dye – The suit was dyed with RIT® dye after construction. Light colors are preferred to avoid color variations.
- Thread to match fabric
- XS – MD = 1-3/8 yards interfacing
- LG – 4XL = 1-3/4 yards interfacing
- 7 Buttons (5/8")
- Basic sewing supplies

Pattern Pieces

- Long Sleeve Jacket Front
- Long Sleeve Jacket Back
- Long Sleeve Jacket Sleeve
- Long Sleeve Jacket Front Band and Facing
- Long Sleeve Jacket Back Facing

Cutting the Pieces

Refer to the layout for the placement of the pattern pieces on the linens (page 31) Note the variation on the bottom of the jacket fronts, the trim on the towel will be used to finish the front edge of the band and facing. The trim on the towels will be the finished edge of the skirt and jacket, therefore the hem line will be placed on the finished edge of the towel and not cut. Notice that there is a separate layout for sizes XS – XL and for 2XL – 4XL.

Purchased Linen Towel Jacket

Purchased Linen Towel Skirt

Unlined Tank

—Directions—

1. Refer to steps 1-4 in the Long Sleeve Jacket General Directions. In step 5, match the neck edge of the facing and the jacket front. Start stitching at the neck edge down to the trim on the towel front (*fig. 1*). Leave the excess facing hanging on the wrong side.
2. Refer to steps 6-8 in the Long Sleeve Jacket General Directions.
3. Fold the extended towel edge back on itself and pin at the angle (*fig. 2*).
4. Flip the extended towel edge up and pin along the front band of the jacket. Pin in place and press well. Zigzag the trim in place (*fig. 3*).
5. Trim the excess front band and facing from behind the trim (*fig. 4*).
6. On the right side, stitch on the fold line of the miter (*fig. 5*). Trim away the excess triangle of the miter (*fig. 6*).
7. Refer to step 9 in the Long Sleeve Jacket General Directions.
8. Refer to step 14 in the Long Sleeve Jacket General Directions.
9. Refer to step 17 in the Long Sleeve Jacket General Directions.
10. Refer to steps 21 and 22 Long Sleeve Jacket General Directions.

Skirt

To determine the size of each skirt panel complete the following steps:

a. Take your hip measurement.

b. Add 6-1/2" to this measurement.

c. Divide this total by 2.

Example: 40" (hip measurement) plus 6-1/2" equals 46-1/2" divided by 2 equals 23-1/4".

Note: We have given directions for side slits in both sides of the skirt. You may make one side slit if you wish.

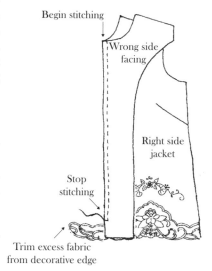

Figure 1

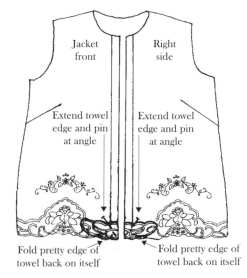

Figure 2

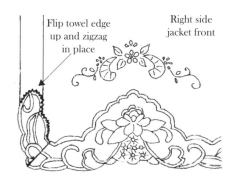

Figure 3

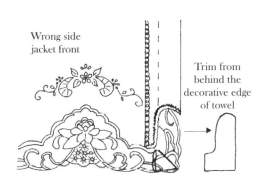

Figure 4

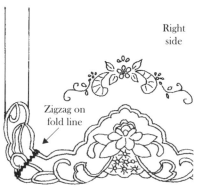

Figure 5

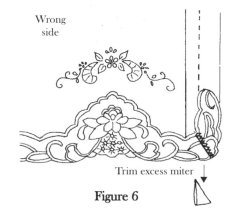

Figure 6

Construction for sizes XS - XL

Two towels (28" by 41") will make a skirt size up to approximately an XL.

1. Use the layout in figure 7 to cut the skirt panels centering the measurement on each towel. Cut the excess from each side.

2. Determine the finished length you would like to have for the skirt. Add 2" to this measurement. Cut the towel length to this measurement *(fig. 7)*.

3. Finish both sides of each panel with a zigzag or serger. If using a serger cut only a scant amount away *(fig. 8)*.

4. With right sides together sew the side seams with a 5/8" seam starting 13" up from the finished hem *(fig. 9)*. Press the seam open for the entire length of the side seam *(fig. 10)*.

5. Stitch the seam allowance of the opening in place staring at the hemline up to seam and back down again 1/2" from the folded edge *(fig. 11)*.

6. Finish the top edge of the skirt by turning 1/4" to the wrong side and press in place. Turn the top edge to the wrong side again 7/8". Stitch close to the folded edge to form the elastic casing *(fig. 12)* leaving 1" unstitched through which to insert the elastic.

7. Fit elastic around waist and cut to fit allowing 1" for overlapping. Run the elastic through the casing and secure the ends together by overlapping 1/2" and stitching through both layers several times. Stitch the 1" opening closed.

Construction for sizes 2XL – 4XL

Three towels (28" by 41") will be required for sizes 2XL – 4XL.

1. Trim away the narrow hemmed edge of each towel.

2. Seam the three towels together removing excess width as desired. Finish the seams. It will not be necessary to have a side or back kick pleat when using three towels.

3. Finish the top edge of the skirt by turning 1/4" to the wrong side and press in place. Turn the top edge to the wrong side again 7/8". Stitch close to the folded edge to form the elastic casing *(see fig. 12)* leave 1" unstitched through which to insert the elastic.

4. Fit elastic around waist and cut to fit allowing 1" for overlapping. Run the elastic through the casing and secure the ends together by overlapping 1/2" and stitching through both layers several times. Stitch the 1" opening closed.

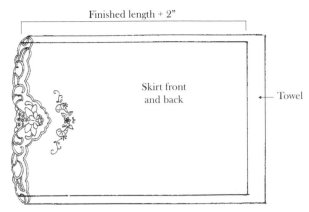

Finished length + 2"

Skirt front and back

Towel

Figure 7

Zigzag or serge

Skirt front

Zigzag or serge

Zigzag or serge

Skirt back

Zigzag or serge

Figure 8

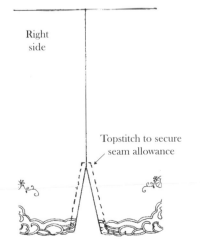

13"

Begin stitching here

Wrong side skirt

Begin stitching here

13" **Figure 9**

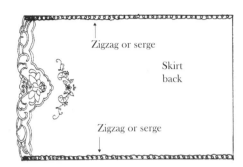

Press side seam open

Wrong side of skirt

Figure 10

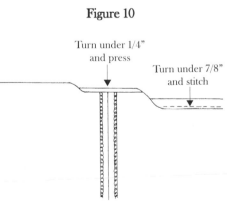

Turn under 1/4" and press

Turn under 7/8" and stitch

Figure 12

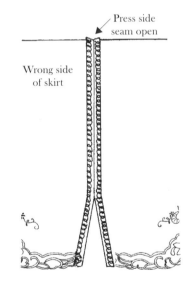

Right side

Topstitch to secure seam allowance

Figure 11

Cutting Layout for Purchased Linen Towel Suit

LAYOUT FOR SLEEVES AND BACK NECK FACING

All sizes

2 Towels

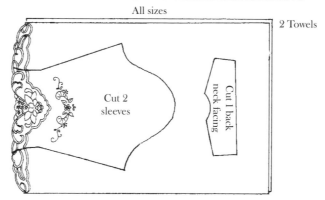

Cut 2 sleeves

Cut 1 back neck facing

LAYOUT FOR SIZES XS - XL

2 towels

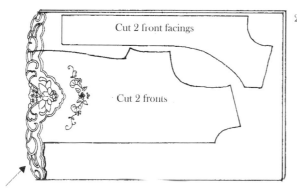

Cut 2 front facings

Cut 2 fronts

Keep this part of the fronts

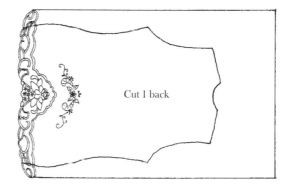

Cut 1 back

LAYOUT FOR SIZES 2XL - 4XL

Cut center of extra towel

Cut 1 front band and facing

2 towels

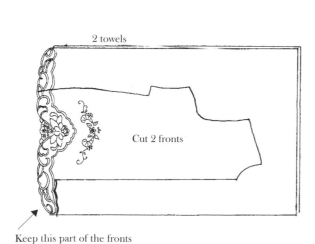

Cut 2 fronts

Keep this part of the fronts

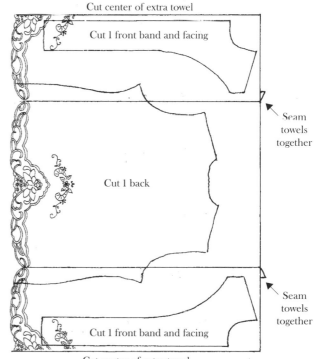

Seam towels together

Cut 1 back

Cut 1 front band and facing

Seam towels together

Cut center of extra towel

Pink Linen Gore Skirt

Beautiful pink linen, ecru handkerchiefs, antique ecru laces and an interesting print fabric of dusty pinks, lavenders and browns are combined in this perfectly elegant skirt. The gore skirt is the pointed version. All of the seams in this outfit are finished using a bias binding on the outside. Even the bottom hem of the skirt has this bias binding finish using the fabulous print fabric trim. At the bottom of each gore, the bias binding is tied in a little knot to finish the end.

Ecru handkerchiefs are stitched around the elasticized waistline of the skirt, and bias binding finishes the top edge of the skirt waistline. The antique ecru laces are pinstitched to the skirt using a wing needle. Marlis Bennett of Bernina of America made this creative outfit that is just perfect for summer occasions.

- This skirt was made with reference to the Gore Skirt General Directions found on page 12.

Note: Some machines have a bias binder attachment which may be used to construct the skirt in place of making your own double-fold bias binding.

Supplies

- For fabric requirements, see Gore Skirt General Directions
- 2 yards of a contrasting fabric for bias
- Four 11"-12" embroidered handkerchiefs for sizes XS - LG and five 11"-12" embroidered handkerchief for sizes XL - 4XL. Note: Handkerchiefs need to have matching embroidery on 2 opposite corners. Most handkerchiefs come in white but may be dyed ecru to coordinate with the fabric you are using.
- 12 yards of 3/4" lace insertion to match handkerchiefs
- Thread to match fabric, handkerchiefs and contrasting bias
- 1 yard of 3/4" wide elastic for sizes XS - LG and 1-1/2 yards of 3/4" wide elastic for sizes XL - 4XL
- 3/4" bias tape maker
- #100 wing needle or #120 universal needle for pinstitching
- Tear-away stabilizer
- Basic sewing supplies

Pattern Pieces

- Gore Skirt Panel

Cutting the Pieces
(refer to layout)

- Cut eight skirt panels. Mark the fold line for the casing at the top of each gore.
- Cut a piece of elastic the following measurement:
  XS - LG - 1 yard
  XL - 4XL -1-1/2 yards
- Cut enough bias strips 1-1/2" wide from the contrasting fabric for each gore seam, each gore hem, and top edge of skirt.

* All seams are stitched 5/8" and trimmed to 1/4" unless otherwise noted.

—Directions—

1. Place each gore on a flat surface and place the lace insertion in a diagonal pattern on each gore. We used approximately 1 to 1-1/2 yards of lace per gore. The lace patterns on the gores should not match and should be random *(fig. 1)*. Pin the lace in place.

Pink Linen Gore Skirt

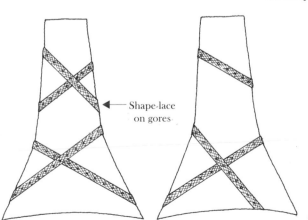

← Shape lace on gores

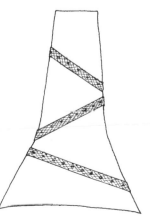

Figure 1

2. Place stabilizer beneath the gore fabric and pinstitch (L=2.5, W=2.5) the edges of the lace to the fabric. The straight portion of the pinstitch should fall on the fabric and the "fingers" of the pinstitch should catch the heading of the lace. **DO NOT** trim fabric from behind the lace *(fig. 2)*. Remove the stabilizer. A small zigzag may be used in place of the pinstitch if desired. Trim all lace ends even with the raw edges of the material.

3. Stitch the bias strips together to make one continuous length of bias.

4. Press the bias following the instructions included with the bias tape maker. Fold the strip of bias tape in half lengthwise and press creating double-fold bias tape.

5. Trim 1/2" from the bottom edge of each gore *(fig. 3)*.

6. Stitch the bias binding to the hemline of each gore as follows:

   a. Unfold one side of the double-fold biastape and pin right sides together along the bottom edge of each gore matching the raw edges of the bias tape and the raw edges of the gore. Allow approximately 1" of bias tape to extend beyond each side of the gore.

   b. Stitch the bias tape to the gore in the unfolded crease of the tape (approximately 1/4") *(fig. 4)*. Clip the seam allowance.

   c. Press the bias binding away from the gore, around the seam allowance and let the fold of the bias binding meet the stitching line on the wrong side of the gore. Pin the binding in place.

   d. Stitch the binding in place, stitching through all layers near the folded edge of the bias strip *(fig. 5)*.

   e. Trim away the excess bias on each side of the gore following the diagonal of the skirt line *(see fig. 5)*.

7. With **wrong** sides together, stitch the gores together with 5/8" seams to form a circle. Trim the seam allowances to 1/4" *(fig. 6)*.

8. Cover the gore seam allowances with the bias tape as follows allowing 2" to extend below the bottom edge of each gore seam:

   a. Unfold one side of the double fold biatape and pin right sides together matching the raw edges of the bias tape to the raw edges of the seam allowance.

   b. Stitch the bias tape to the seam allowance in the unfolded crease of the tape (1/4") *(fig. 7)*.

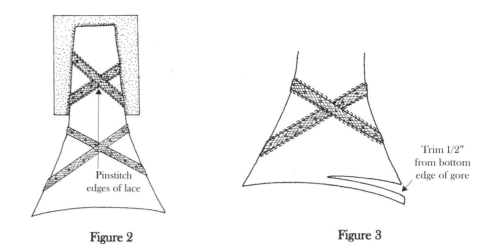

Pinstitch edges of lace

Figure 2

Trim 1/2" from bottom edge of gore

Figure 3

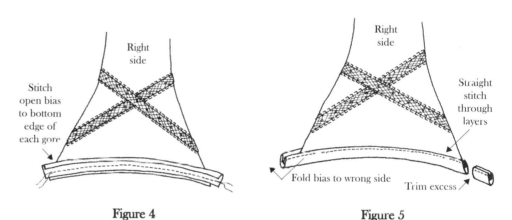

Stitch open bias to bottom edge of each gore

Right side

Figure 4

Right side

Straight stitch through layers

Fold bias to wrong side

Trim excess

Figure 5

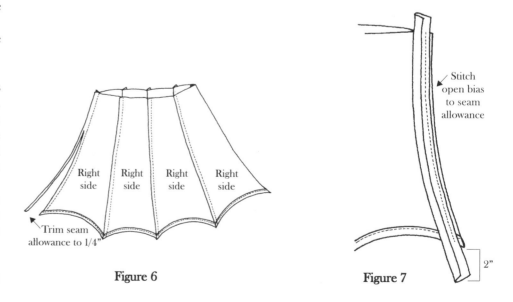

Right side   Right side   Right side   Right side

Trim seam allowance to 1/4"

Figure 6

Stitch open bias to seam allowance

2"

Figure 7

c. Press the bias binding away from the gore, around the seam allowance and let the fold of the bias binding meet the stitching line on the back of the seam allowance. Pin the binding in place.

d. Stitch the binding in place stitching through all layers near the folded edge of the bias strip. Trim away the excess binding at the waistline *(fig. 8)*.

9. At the hemline, tie a knot in the 2" extension, sliding the knot very close to the edge of the finished hem. Leave a 1/2" tail past the knot and cut away the excess bias *(fig. 9)*.

10. Cut the handkerchiefs at a diagonal to create triangles (8 for sizes XS – LG and 10 for sizes XL – 4XL).

11. Place the cut edge of each handkerchief triangle even with the drawn fold line of the casing at the waist of the skirt. Pin in place. The handkerchiefs will overlap each other around the circumference of the skirt. Adjust the overlap of the handkerchiefs as needed to be approximately equal.

12. Stitch 1/4" from the cut edge of the handkerchiefs. With a wide zigzag, stitch the raw edges of the handkerchiefs in place *(fig. 10)*.

13. Serge or overcast the top raw edge of the skirt *(fig. 10)*.

14. Fold a casing in place along the fold line and pin in place.

15. Stitch the casing 1-1/4" from the top edge fold stitching close to the edge of the overcast leaving 1" of the casing unstitched *(fig. 11)*.

16. Press the casing well.

17. Cover the top fold of the casing with the bias tape as follows:

a. Unfold one side of the double fold bias tape. Begin at the center back, fold 1/4" to the wrong side and pin right sides together matching the raw edges of the bias tape to the top folded edge of the casing.

b. Stitch the bias tape to all layers of the casing by stitching in the unfolded crease of the tape (1/4") *(fig. 12)*.

c. Press the bias binding away from the skirt, around the top edge of the casing and let the fold of the bias binding meet the stitching line on the inside of the casing. Pin the binding in place.

d. Stitch the binding in place stitching through all layers near the folded edge of the bias strip. The bias strip should cover the raw edges of the handkerchiefs *(fig. 13)*.

18. Thread the elastic through the casing formed in the top of the skirt. Pull the elastic through the casing. Pin the ends together with a safety pin.

19. Try on the skirt and overlap the elastics to a comfortable fit. Stitch approximately 1" of the overlap and trim away any excess elastic from each end *(fig. 14)*.

20. Stretch the elastic so that the overlap slips into the casing. Stitch the 1" opening closed.

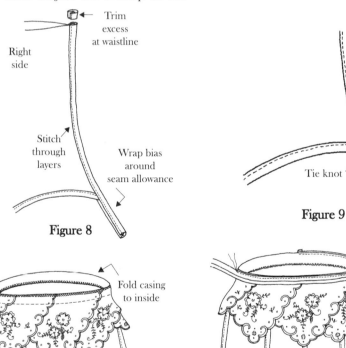

Trim excess at waistline

Right side

Stitch through layers

Wrap bias around seam allowance

Figure 8

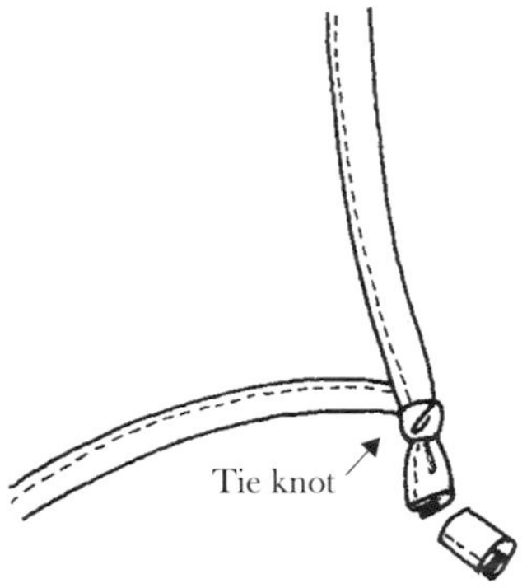

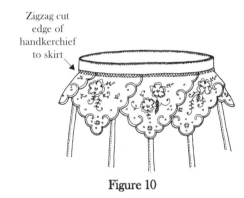

Tie knot

Figure 9

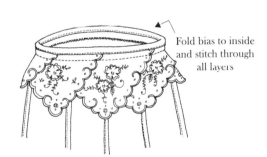

Zigzag cut edge of handkerchief to skirt

Figure 10

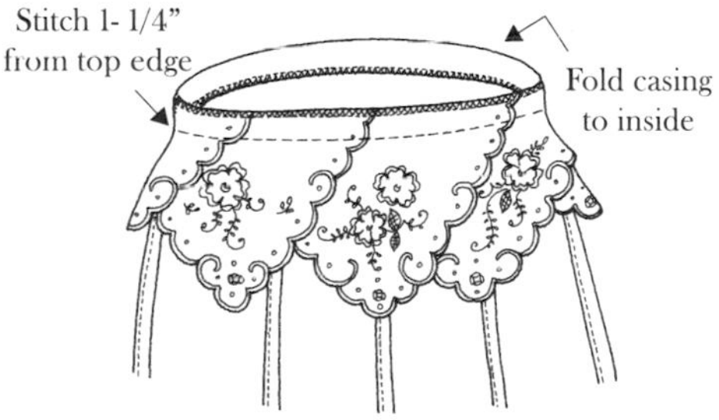

Stitch 1-1/4" from top edge

Fold casing to inside

Figure 11

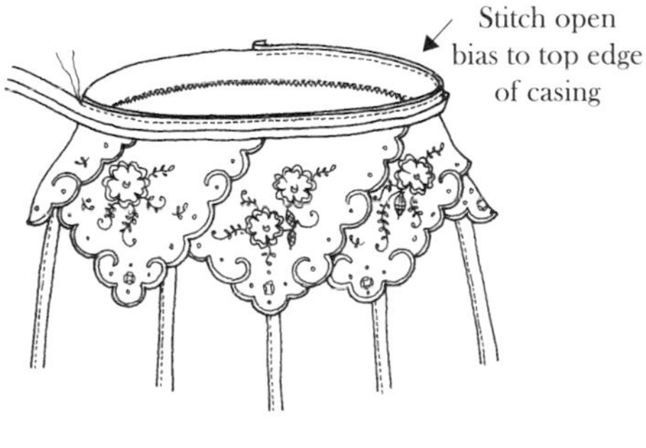

Stitch open bias to top edge of casing

Figure 12

Fold bias to inside and stitch through all layers

Figure 13

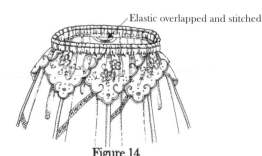

Elastic overlapped and stitched

Figure 14

Pink Linen Tank

Beautiful pink linen, ecru handkerchiefs, antique ecru laces and an interesting print fabric of dusty pinks, lavenders and browns are combined in this perfectly elegant tank. All of the seams in this outfit are finished using a bias binding on the outside. Even the bottom hem of the tank has this bias binding finish using the fabulous print fabric trim. At the bottom of each side of the tank the bias binding is tied in a little knot to finish the end.

An ecru handkerchief is straight stitched to the front of the tank. Marlis Bennett of Bernina of America made this creative outfit that is just perfect for summer occasions.

- This tank with this outfit was made with reference to the Tank General Directions found on page 3.

Note: Some machines have a bias binder attachment which may be used to construct the tank in place of making your own double fold bias binding.

Supplies

- For fabric requirements, see Tank General Directions
- 1 yard of a contrasting fabric for bias, this will allow ample fabric to avoid a lot of piecing
- One 11"-12" handkerchief for the front of the tank. Note: Most handkerchiefs come in white but may be dyed ecru to coordinate with the fabric you are using.
- Thread to match fabric, handkerchief and contrasting bias
- 3/4" bias tape maker
- Basic sewing supplies

Pattern Pieces

- Tank Front
- Tank Back

Cutting the Pieces

(refer to the layout for the Tank General Directions)

- Cut one tank front on the fold—remove 5/8" seam allowance from the neck edge and armhole edges
- Cut one tank back on the fold—remove 5/8" seam allowance from the neck edge and armhole edges
- Cut enough bias 1-1/2" wide to go around the neck, the two armholes, across the hem of the front and back of the tank and down each side plus 3" for extensions
- Optional: Mark the darts in the tank front

* All seams are stitched 5/8" and trimmed to 1/4" unless otherwise noted.

—Directions—

1. Stitch bias strips together to make one continuous length of bias (*fig. 1*).
2. Stitch the optional fit darts in the tank front if desired.
3. Place handkerchief, with the wrong side of handkerchief to the right side of the tank front adjusting it to fit (*fig. 2*). Note: The corners of the handkerchief will extend past the armhole curves on the smaller sizes and will not reach the armhole curves on the larger sizes.
4. With thread to match the handkerchief, stitch very close to the edge of the handkerchief, attaching it to the tank front (*fig. 2*).
5. Trim the excess handkerchief from the armhole curves and neckline and stitch very close to the raw edges through both layers (*fig. 3*). The tank front and handkerchief overlay will now be treated as one piece.

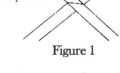

Figure 1

Pink Linen Tank

Right side handkerchief overlay

Figure 2

Cut away excess

Figure 3

6. With **wrong** sides of the tank together, stitch the shoulder seams. Trim the shoulder seams to 1/4" *(fig. 4)*.

7. Press the bias tape following the instructions included with the bias tape maker. Fold the strip of bias tape in half lengthwise and press creating double-fold bias tape.

8. Cover the shoulder seams with the bias tape as follows:

   a. Unfold one side of the double-fold bias tape and pin right sides together matching the raw edges of the bias tape to the raw edges of the shoulder seam.

   b. Stitch the bias tape to the shoulder seam in the unfolded crease of the tape (1/4") *(fig. 5)*.

   c. Press the bias binding away from the tank, around the seam allowance, and let the fold of the bias binding meet the stitching line on the back of the seam allowance. Pin the binding in place.

   d. Stitch the binding in place stitching through all layers near the folded edge of the bias strip *(fig. 6)*.

9. Press the bias covered seam allowance toward the back of the tank *(fig. 7)*.

10. Stitch the binding to the neckline as follows:

    a. Unfold one side of the double-fold bias tape and pin right sides together along the neck edge beginning at the center back, folding up 1/4" at the start. Match the raw edges of the bias tape and the raw edges of the tank neck edge. Be sure the shoulder seams stay pressed toward the back of the garment *(fig. 8)*.

    b. Stitch the bias tape to the tank in the unfolded crease of the tape (approximately 1/4") *(fig. 8)*. Clip the seam allowance.

    c. Press the bias binding away from the tank, around the seam allowance. and let the fold of the bias binding meet the stitching line on the wrong side of the tank. Pin the binding in place.

    d. Stitch the binding in place, stitching through all layers at the folded edge of the bias strip *(fig. 9)*.

11. Stitch the bias binding to the armholes following steps 10a-10d above; starting at one side seam, stitch around the curve to the other side seam. The 1/4" turn under in step 10a will not be needed at this edge. Trim the binding even with the side of the tank *(fig. 10)*.

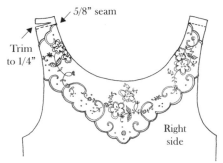

5/8" seam
Trim to 1/4"
Right side

Figure 4

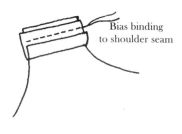

Bias binding to shoulder seam

Figure 5

Handkerchief is not pictured in Figures 6-13

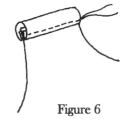

Figure 6

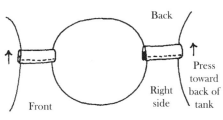

Back
Press toward back of tank
Right side
Front

Figure 7

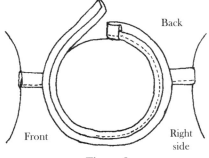

Back
Front
Right side

Figure 8

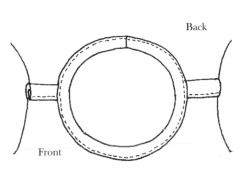

Back
Front

Figure 9

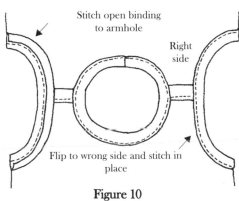

Stitch open binding to armhole
Right side
Flip to wrong side and stitch in place

Figure 10

12. Attach binding to the bottom edge of the tank front and the tank back following steps 10a-10d. Since you are stitching along a straight hemline, you will not need to turn under 1/4" at the start (10a) nor clip the seam allowance in step 10b *(fig. 11)*. Trim binding even with the side of the tank.

13. With **wrong** sides of the tank together stitch the side seams. Trim the seam to 1/4" *(fig. 12)*.

14. Cover the 1/4" side seam allowances by following steps 8a-8d, allowing 1" of bias to extend at the underarm and 2" of bias to extend at the hemline *(fig. 13)*.

15. Press the covered seam allowance toward the back of the tank and fold the bias extension to the inside of the tank at the armhole curve. Stitch in place and trim away the excess bias.

16. At the hemline, tie a knot in the 2" extension, sliding the knot very close to the edge of the finished hem. Leave a 1/2" tail past the knot and cut away the excess bias *(fig. 14)*.

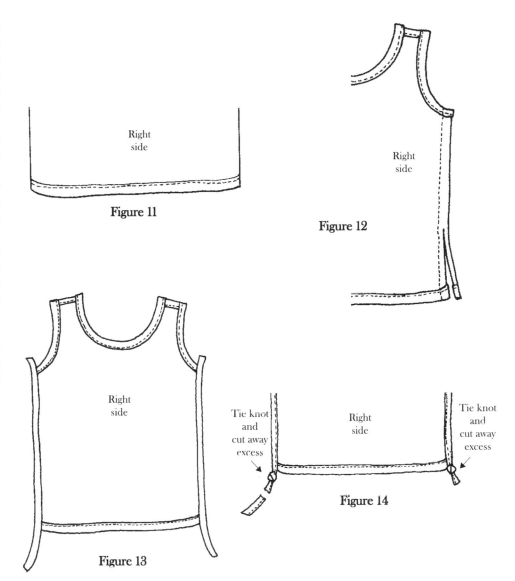

Figure 11

Figure 12

Figure 13

Figure 14

Women's Size Chart

Size	2-4 XS	6-8 SM	10-12 MD	14-16 LG	18-20 XL	22-24 2XL	26-28 3XL	30-32 4XL
BUST	31	34	37	40	44	48	52	56
WAIST	23	26	29	32	36	40	44	48
HIP	33	36	39	42	46	50	54	58

Gray Kimono Jacket with Organza Trim

This gray suit might come straight from the fashion pages of a Paris couturier magazine. Made of a gray and beige polka dot rayon fabric, the tank top features a double-layered strip of beige organza at the bottom edge. The bias skirt is made with the fashion fabric. The kimono jacket is simple and elegant, with the pockets featuring a double-folded piece of beige organza at the top. Beautiful decorative pearl buttons are used to close the front of the suit. The back of the suit has a casing with bias tubes of the fashion fabric run through and tied in the center to pull in part of the fullness of the jacket.

- This jacket was made with reference to the Kimono Jacket General Directions found on page 14.
- The skirt was made by the Bias Skirt General Directions found on page 10.

Supplies

- Refer to the fabric requirements for the Kimono Jacket, adding 1/4 yard to fabric yardage
- 1/4 yard of sheer fabric for trim
- Thread to match fabric
- One yard interfacing
- 5 buttons (3/4") for the jacket front
- 6 buttons (5/8") – three for each sleeve (optional)
- Basic sewing supplies

* All seams are 5/8" unless otherwise noted. To finish seam, trim seam to 1/4" and overcast edge by machine or serger.

Pattern Pieces

- Refer to the pattern pieces needed in the Kimono Jacket General Directions

Note: The pictured jacket omits the sleeve cuff. If you wish to construct the jacket minus the cuff, cut the sleeves 4" longer.

Cutting the Pieces

- Refer to the Kimono Jacket General Directions and cut the pieces listed. Be sure to lengthen the sleeve if omitting the cuff
- Cut a 1-1/2" by 36" strip of fabric for the back casing
- Cut two strips for the back cording 1-1/4" by 30"
- Cut two pieces 7" long by 7-3/4" wide for the fabric portion of the pockets
- Cut two pieces 5" long by 7-3/4" wide for the sheer portion of the pockets

—Directions—

1. Refer to the Kimono Jacket instructions, steps 1 – 6 and complete the steps.
2. For the casing and cording in the back, complete the following steps:
   a. To make the casing, turn under 1/4" along each long side of the strip creating a strip 1" wide *(fig. 1)*.
   b. Measure up 13-1/2" from the bottom edge of the jacket back and draw a line straight across *(fig. 2)*. You may alter this measurement as needed to fit your waistline.
   c. Fold the jacket back in half and mark the center back at the line drawn in step 2-b.
   d. On the right side of the jacket, stitch two 5/8" buttonholes just below the drawn line spacing them 1/2" on each side of the center back *(fig. 2)*. Cut the buttonholes open.
   e. Place the casing fabric on the wrong side of the jacket back, placing the top edge of the casing along the drawn line. Stitch the casing to the jacket back very close to the top and bottom edges of the casing *(fig. 3)*.

Gray Kimono Jacket with Organza Trim

Figure 1

Figure 2

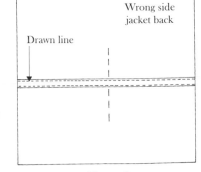

Figure 3

f. Fold each cording strip right sides together. Stitch across one end and down the side with a 1/4" seam *(fig. 4)*. Turn the cording right side out.

g. Run the cording through the casing with the finished ends hanging from the buttonholes in the center back of the jacket. Secure the ends of the cording at the jacket back side seam lines *(fig. 5)*.

3. Embellish the pockets as follows:

   a. Press the two sheer pieces in half to measure 2-1/2" by 7-3/4" *(fig. 6)*.

   b. Stitch the long raw edges to the top edge of each pocket with a 5/8" seam. Trim and finish the seam *(fig. 7)* and press the seam toward the solid fabric.

   c. Secure the seam in place by stitching the seam to the fabric 1/4" from the seam line. Serge or overcast both sides and the bottom edge of each pocket *(fig. 8)*.

   d. Press under 5/8" along the two sides and bottom of each pocket *(fig. 9)*.

4. Position the pockets on the jacket fronts about 3-1/2" from the bottom edge and 2" from the side edge of the jacket fronts. Stitch the pockets to the jacket front close to the three finished edges *(fig. 10)*.

5. Refer to the Kimono Jacket General Directions, and complete steps 7 – 14.

6. Finish the hemline of the sleeves by using one of the following methods:

Hemmed sleeve with no cuff

1. Finish the edge of the lengthened sleeve with a serge or overcast *(fig. 11)*.

2. Turn under a 1" hem and pin in place.

3. Top stitch the hem in place 3/4" from the folded edge *(fig. 12)*.

4. Attach three buttons on each sleeve spaced approximately 1/2" apart (see finished drawing).

Cuffed version

Refer to the Kimono Jacket General Directions and complete steps 15 – 17 to attach the cuff.

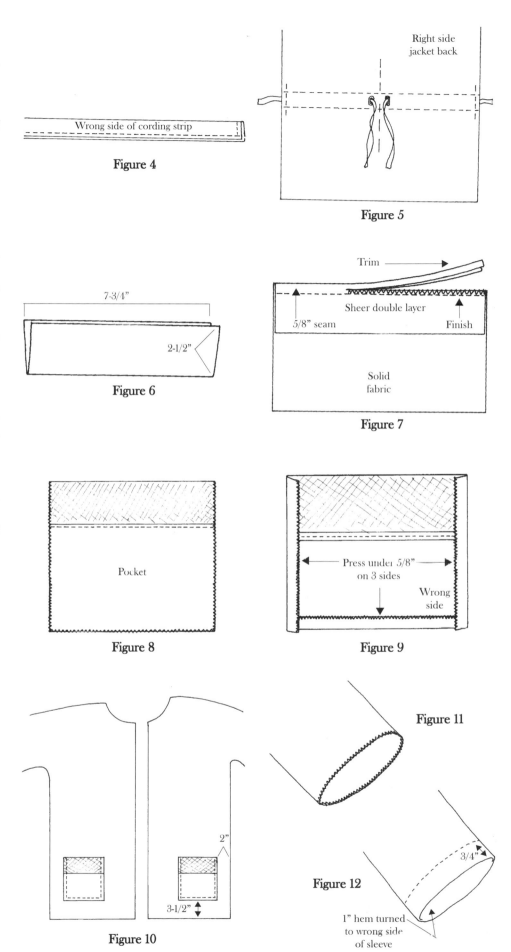

Wrong side of cording strip

Figure 4

Right side jacket back

Figure 5

7-3/4"

2-1/2"

Figure 6

Trim

Sheer double layer

5/8" seam

Finish

Solid fabric

Figure 7

Pocket

Figure 8

Press under 5/8" on 3 sides

Wrong side

Figure 9

Figure 11

Figure 12

2"

3-1/2"

Figure 10

3/4"

1" hem turned to wrong side of sleeve

Gray Tank

This tank top is a wonderful addition to the gray jacket and skirt when you want a three-piece suit with matching fabrics. It features a double-layered strip of beige organza at the bottom edge. This technique is so easy and can be incorporated into many garments.

- This tank was made with reference to the Tank General Directions - Bias Facing Version found on page 3.

Supplies

- For fabric requirements, see Tank General Directions
- 1/2 yard of sheer fabric for lower edge of tank
- Sewing thread to match the fabric
- 1/2" bias tape maker
- Basic sewing supplies

* All seams are 5/8" unless otherwise noted. To finish seam, trim seam to 1/4" and overcast edge by machine or serger.

Pattern Pieces

- Tank Front (shorten the pattern 5")
- Tank Back (shorten the pattern 5")

Cutting the Pieces

(refer to the layout)

- Cut one tank front on the fold and one tank back on the fold from the tank fabric using the shortened pattern
- Cut enough bias 1" wide to go around the neck and the two armholes
- Optional: Mark the darts in the tank front

—Directions—

1. Refer to the Tank General Directions - Unlined Version with Bias Facings and complete steps 1 - 13. Do not hem the tank at this time.
2. Measure across the tank front along the bottom edge from side seam to side seam. Add 1" to this measurement. Call this measurement "A" (*fig. 1*).
3. Cut a rectangle of fabric 7" by "A" across the fabric (*fig. 2*). Do not include the selvage in this measurement.
4. Fold the rectangle of fabric in half right sides together to create a piece 3-1/2" by "A".
5. Stitch a 1/2" seam along each end of the piece. Trim the seam allowance to 1/4" (*fig. 3*).
6. Turn the piece right side out and press matching the raw edges.
7. Place the sheer panel to the right side of the tank front matching the raw edges of the sheer panel to the raw edge of the bottom tank front. Pin in place (*fig. 4*).
8. Repeat steps 2 - 7 for the bottom edge of the tank back.
9. Stitch around the bottom edge of the tank with a 1/2" seam. Finish the seam with a serge or overcast (*fig. 5*).
10. Press the seam allowance toward the tank. Topstitch the seam allowance in place 1/4" from the seam line around the tank front and back (*fig. 6*).

**Gray Tank
with Organdy Trim**

Tank front

A

Figure 1

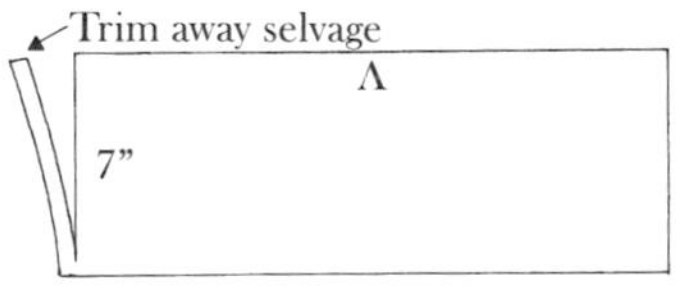

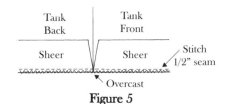

Trim away selvage

A

7"

Figure 2

Stitch 1/2" seam

3-1/2"

Trim seam to 1/4"

Figure 3

Tank front

Figure 4

Tank Back | Tank Front

Sheer | Sheer

Stitch 1/2" seam

Overcast

Figure 5

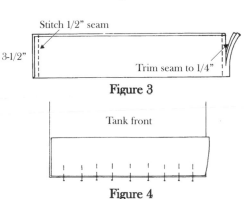

Tank front

Topstitch

Figure 6

Green Silk Kimono Jacket

Using a dusty green silk dupioni, Lindee Goodall of Cactus Punch created an interesting jacket using machine appliqué. The leaves of a green silk fabric darker than the jacket are machine appliquéd, a technique that goes very quickly since it is outlined as it is attached. The peach flower on the front has two layers. The bottom layer is stitched and applied to the jacket with a little zigzag, overlapping the leaves. The second layer is made of individual flowers stitched and cut out, then applied with only a pearl in the middle to attach them to the first peach flowered layer. The front placket has bias piping on either side and the buttons are covered with self-fabric. The sleeves are finished with a cuff.

- This jacket was made with reference to the Kimono Jacket General Directions found on page 14.

Pattern Pieces & Cutting

- For the Pattern Pieces Needed and Cutting the Pieces, refer to the Kimono Jacket General Directions
- Optional leaf design
- From the remaining 1/3 yard of jacket fabric, cut 1-3/8" wide bias strips that when sewn together will equal at least 3 yards of bias. Refer to the technique for Making Piping and make three yards of bias piping for the jacket.

* All seams are 5/8" unless otherwise noted. To finish the seam, trim the seam to 1/4" and overcast edge by machine or serger.

The floral embroidery on the jacket is an adaptation of the Forget-Me-Nots, Signature 20 disk. The leaves are from Poinsettia Bract, Signature 4. Both disks are available from Cactus Punch. You may use this design or choose other floral and leaf embroidery designs. A leaf design is included at the end of the instructions if you wish to trace a design. Applique instructions are given in the directions section of this garment embellishment section.

Supplies

- Refer to the fabric yardage in the Kimono Jacket General Directions adding 1/3 yard for making piping
- Sewing thread to match the jacket fabric
- One yard of interfacing
- Two 12" squares of contrasting fabric (peach) for the flower appliqués
- Two 12" squares of contrasting fabric (green) for leaf appliqués
- Tear away stabilizer
- KK2000™

- Decorative thread to match both the flower and leaf fabrics
- Designs listed previously (available from Cactus Punch) or you may choose another comparable design
- 6mm pearls to sew in the centers of the flowers
- 3 yards of cording for making piping
- Five 7/8" covered buttons
- Basic sewing supplies

Green Silk Kimono Jacket

Completing the Machine Appliqué Embroidery

1. With stabilizer beneath a square of fabric hoop and stitch the embroidered flower design *(fig. 1)*.
2. Trim close to the edge with small scissors. Be very careful not to cut the threads *(fig. 2)*.
3. Repeat step 1 for the second square of fabric. Trim very close to the satin stitching to create several single flowers *(fig. 3)*.

—Directions—

1. Position the machine appliqué embroidered flower design on the jacket left or right front *(fig. 4)*.
2. Determine positioning for the leaves and stem (the flower embroidery will cover portions of some of the leaves). Draw the leaves and stem onto the jacket front. Remove the flower embroidery *(fig. 5)*.
3. Trace the leaf design onto the green fabric. With KK2000™, adhere the square of green fabric over the leaf area on the jacket. Stitch the first small zigzag around the leaves *(fig. 6)*. Trim the green fabric close to the stitching. Satin stitch around the leaves to complete *(fig. 7)*.
4. Stitch the veins in the leaves with a machine straight stitch *(fig. 8)*.
5. Complete the stem with a satin stitch *(see fig. 7)*.
6. Place the flower design in position and stitch around the edge with a small zigzag and matching or invisible thread *(fig. 9)*.
7. Attach the freestanding flowers randomly on top of the floral design on the jacket by stitching only in the middle of the flower, leaving edges free. Add a decorative pearl in the middle of each attached flower.
8. Refer to the Kimono Jacket construction steps 1 - 3.
9. Stitch piping to one side of each front band *(fig. 10)*. Attach this side of the band (the one with the piping) to the two front edges of the jacket.
10. Finish the remaining side of the bands by turning under 5/8". With wrong sides together, fold the bands along the fold line creating a front band and band facing. Press.

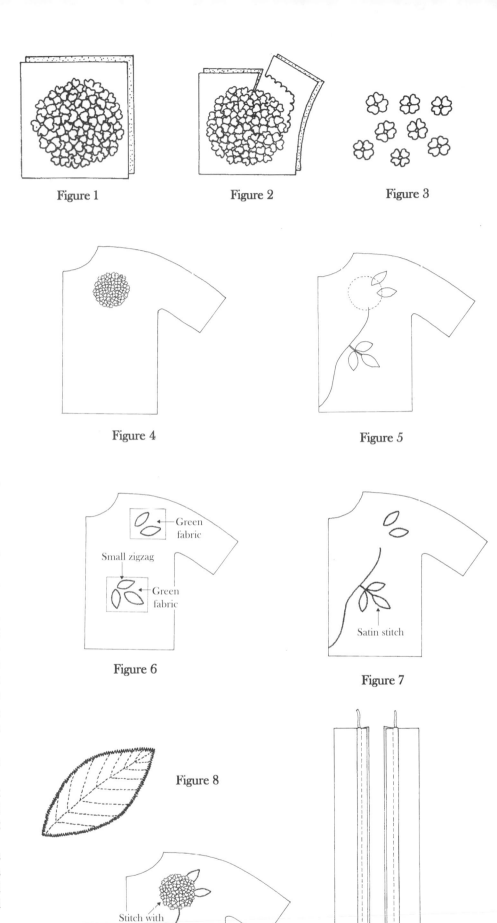

Figure 1

Figure 2

Figure 3

Figure 4

Figure 5

Green fabric

Small zigzag

Green fabric

Figure 6

Satin stitch

Figure 7

Figure 8

Stitch with invisible thread

Figure 9

Figure 10

11. With the band facing opened out, attach piping to the neck edge of the jacket starting at the fold line in the front and leaving 1/4" of the piping extended onto the facing portion of the band. End at the fold line on the other side with the piping extending 1/4" onto the facing portion of the band (*fig. 11*).

12. Fold the front facings on the fold line with right sides together. Finish the outer edge of the neck facing by pressing under 3/8" and topstitch 1/8" from the edge. Place the neck facing to the neck of the jacket with right sides together. The facing will lie on top of the front band facing. Stitch the facing to the jacket at the neck edge, using the piping stitching line as a guide (*fig. 12*). Trim and clip the seam. Turn the neck facings and band facings to the wrong side and press in place. Top stitch the front and back neck edges 1/8" from the seam line catching the facing as you stitch (*fig. 13*).

13. Refer to the Kimono Jacket construction steps 7 - 9.

14. When hemming is complete, press the front facing in place along the fold line. Pin in place. Top stitch 1/8" from each long side of the band catching the facing as you stitch (*fig. 14*).

15. Refer to the Kimono Jacket construction steps 14 – 17. On the silk jacket the cuff may be turned up or left down. Cuff and neck edge may be topstitched if desired.

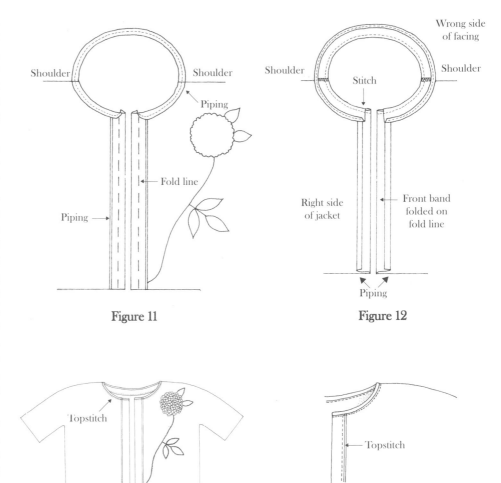

Figure 11

Figure 12

Figure 13

Figure 14

Optional Leaf Design

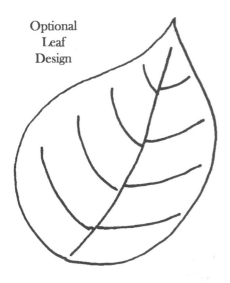

Detail of Green Silk Kimono Jacket

Blue Linen Kimono Jacket

This beautiful blue handkerchief linen jacket has some wonderful machine embroidery techniques. Made by Peggy Dilbone, an educator for Husqvarna/Viking, the jacket has a beautiful large blue embroidery on the upper right-hand shoulder. The sleeve cuffs and front plackets have off-the-edge scalloping and candlewicking. A bias skirt in matching blue linen completes this elegant tone-on-tone suit. This suit is perfect for spring and summer occasions and would be just as elegant in black as in the pastel color. The suit closes with fancy blue flower buttons.

- This jacket was made with reference to the Kimono Jacket General Directions found on page 14.
- The skirt was made by the Bias Skirt General Directions found on page 10.

Note: This shell was embroidered using a Viking Designer I. The large embroidery is from Husqvarna Viking Disk 112, menu 2:5. The off-the-edge scallops are stitched using H-24, side to side mirror with decorative thread in the needle and bobbin. A candlewicking stitch was also used.

* All seams are 5/8" unless otherwise noted. To finish the seam, trim the seam to 1/4" and overcast edge by machine or serger.

Supplies

- Refer to the Kimono Jacket General Directions for the fabric requirements
- 40 wt. decorative thread to match the fabric
- Stitch in the Ditch™ stabilizer
- Tear-away stabilizer
- One yard lightweight interfacing
- Basic sewing supplies

Pattern Pieces

- Refer to the pattern pieces needed in the Kimono Jacket General Directions

Cutting the Pieces

- Refer to the layout on the jacket pattern

—Directions—

1. Position the machine embroidery on the right or left jacket front. Using tear away stabilizer, embroider the jacket using the design listed above or a design of your choice. Remove the stabilizer and press well *(fig. 1)*.
2. Refer to the Kimono Jacket General Directions, steps 1-5 and complete the steps.
3. Finish the outer edge of the neck facing by stitching the folded edge in place. Stitch the neck edge close to the neck line through all layers *(fig. 2)*.
4. Fold 1/2" to the wrong side on one long side of each of the two front bands. Embellish the folded edge with the decorative scallop stitch as listed above or a scallop stitch of your choice *(fig. 3)*.

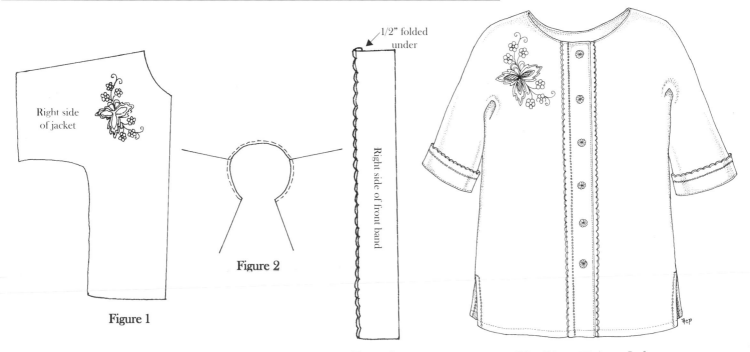

Right side of jacket

Figure 1

Figure 2

1/2" folded under

Right side of front band

Figure 3

Blue Linen Kimono Jacket

• Rust Jacket with
  Ultrasuede™
• Rust Tank
• Bias Skirt.

• Elegant Netting Shell

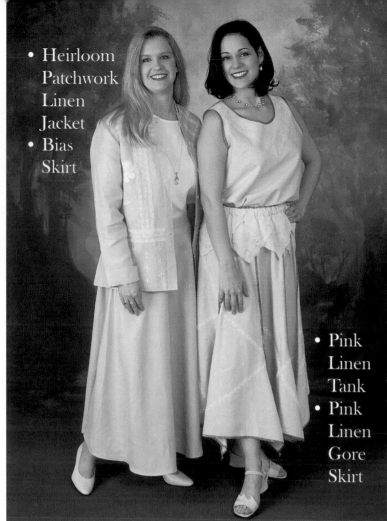

• Heirloom
Patchwork
Linen
Jacket
• Bias
Skirt

• Pink
Linen
Tank
• Pink
Linen
Gore
Skirt

• Purchased Linen
Towel Suit

• Pink Linen
Arizona Jacket
• Bias Skirt

• Instant Appliqué/
Stippled Kimono Jacket
• Lined Tank
• Bias Skirt

• Yellow Silk Ribbon Embroidered Jacket
• Lined Tank   • Gore Skirt

- Gray Kimono Jacket
  with Organza Trim
- Gray Tank with Organza Trim
- Bias Skirt

Green Silk Kimono Jacket

• Blue Linen
Sweet Pea/
Foxglove Shell

• Ecru Linen Iris Shell

• Blue Linen
Kimono Jacket
• Bias Skirt

• Cream Linen
Jacket with
Bobbin Work
Lined Tank
Gore Skirt

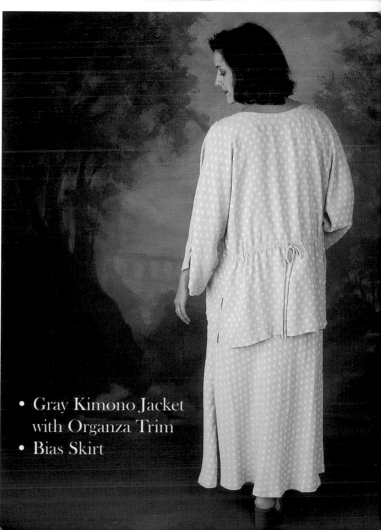

• Gray Kimono Jacket
with Organza Trim
• Bias Skirt

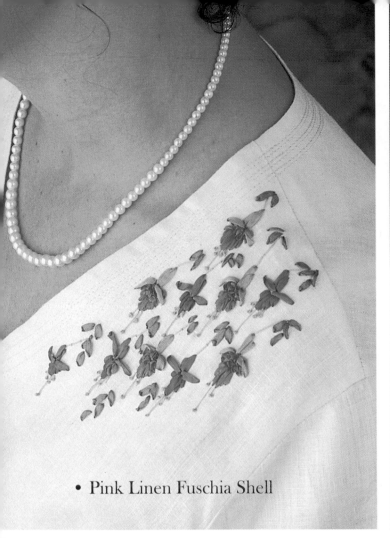

• Pink Linen Fuschia Shell

• Peach Linen
Kimono Jacket
• Bias Skirt

• Circular Embroidered
Jacket, Shell, and Skirt

• Triple Puffing Batiste Shell

• Black and Blue
Color-Blocked
Silk Jacket

• Color-Blocked
Silk Jacket

Jacobean
Embroidered
Shell

• Reverse Embroidery
and Couching Jacket
• Gore Skirt

• Color-Blocked
Long-Sleeve Shell
• Bias Skirt

5. Fold the sleeve band in half wrong sides together with long edges meeting and press. Embellish the folded edge with the decorative scallop stitch as listed above or a scallop stitch of your choice *(fig. 4)*. On the sleeve band stitch a second row of decorative stitching 5/8" from the points of the scallops. We chose a candlewicking stitch or you may use a satin stitch dot *(fig. 4)*.

6. With the right side of the sleeve bands to the wrong side of the sleeves, matching the raw edges, stitch the bands to the sleeves with a 5/8" seam. Trim and finish the seam *(fig. 5)*.

7. With right sides together, place the front to the back at the side and sleeve. Stitch the side and sleeve seam beginning just above the seam attaching the sleeve band and stopping at the dot on the bottom side seam *(fig. 6)*. Clip through the seam allowance to the stitching line on the sleeve end of the side seam. Clip through the seam allowance 1" above the dot on each side. Trim and finish the seam from clip to clip *(fig.6)*.

8. Overcast or serge each raw edge of the side opening at the bottom of the jacket *(fig.7)*.

9. At the clip on the sleeves, pull the seam allowances to the other side so that the sleeve bands are right sides together *(fig. 8)*. Stitch the seam allowance of the bands, trim and finish the seams *(fig.8)*.

10. Fold the bands to the right side of the sleeves and press. Stitch close to the folded edge with a straight stitch to hold the bands in place *(fig.9)*.

11. Refer to the Kimono Jacket General Directions, steps 8 and 9 and complete the steps.

12. Stitch the front band to the jacket front with the right side of the band to the wrong side of the jacket leaving 5/8" of fabric extended above the edge of the neck and the bottom of the jacket *(fig. 10)*. Press the band away from the jacket.

13. Fold the band with wrong sides together to the front. The finished scallop edge will extend over the seam 1/8" *(fig. 11)*. Press the fold line in the front band.

14. Fold the band on the pressed fold to the wrong side of the jacket with right sides of the band together *(fig. 12)*. Stitch across the bottom and the top edge of the band following the finished edge of the jacket *(fig. 12)*. Trim the seam.

15. Flip the band to the right side *(fig. 13)*. Press the top and bottom seam.

16. Stitch the front side of the band in place close to the scalloped edge with a candlewicking stitch or you may use a satin stitch dot *(fig. 13)*.

17. Stitch close to the folded edge with a straight stitch to hold the band in place *(fig.13)*.

18. Refer to the Kimono Jacket General Directions, step 14 and complete the steps.

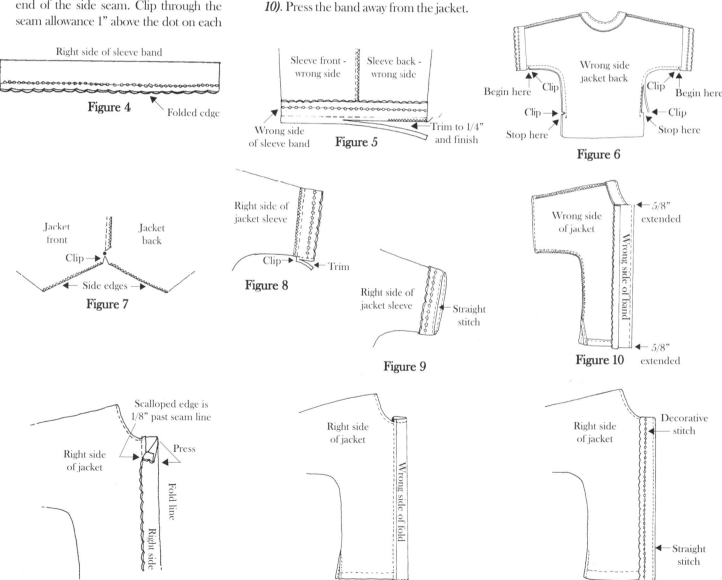

Right side of sleeve band

Figure 4 Folded edge

Sleeve front - wrong side   Sleeve back - wrong side

Wrong side of sleeve band   **Figure 5**   Trim to 1/4" and finish

Wrong side jacket back

Begin here   Clip   Clip   Begin here
Clip   Clip
Stop here   Stop here
Figure 6

Jacket front   Jacket back
Clip
Side edges
Figure 7

Right side of jacket sleeve
Clip   Trim
Figure 8

Right side of jacket sleeve   Straight stitch
Figure 9

Wrong side of jacket   5/8" extended
Wrong side of band
5/8" extended
Figure 10

Scalloped edge is 1/8" past seam line
Right side of jacket   Press
Fold line
Right side
Figure 11

Right side of jacket   Wrong side of fold
Figure 12

Right side of jacket   Decorative stitch
Straight stitch
Figure 13

Peach Linen Kimono Jacket

Using Singer's lace card, Lana Bennett, a Singer educator, stitched lace on this suit in two different ways. The suit is made of a beautiful peach linen; all of the stitching is done in almost the same shade of peach. Machine embroideries stitched on organza create "lace insertion" that is applied with satin stitch around the bottom of the jacket. The same lace design is stitched around the edges of the kimono sleeves. This jacket has an extra front placket to hide the buttons and buttonholes; another pattern from the lace card is used to embellish this placket. The bottom of the bias skirt is embellished with the same lace design.

- This jacket was made with reference to the Kimono Jacket General Directions found on page 14.
- The skirt was made by the Bias Skirt General Directions found on page 10 with an embroidery matching the jacket placed 4-1/4" from the finished hem.

This jacket was embroidered using a Singer XL1000. All embroideries are from the Singer Lace Card IX.

Supplies

- Refer to the Kimono Jacket General Directions for the fabric requirements
- 1/2 yard of organza to match the fabric
- 40 wt. decorative thread to match the fabric
- Wash-away stabilizer (WSS)
- Tear-away stabilizer
- Basic sewing supplies

Pattern Pieces

- Refer to the pattern pieces needed in the Kimono Jacket General Directions

Cutting the Pieces

- Cut one jacket back on the fold
- Cut two jacket fronts
- Cut two jacket sleeve bands
- Cut three jacket front bands from the main fabric
- Cut one jacket front band from the organza
- Cut jacket back facing on the fold
- Cut two jacket front facings
- From the organza cut two strips 4" by width across the bottom of the jacket front and one strip 4" by the width across the jacket back.

* All seams are 5/8" unless otherwise noted. To finish seam, trim seam to 1/4" and overcast edge by machine or serger.

—Directions—

1. Select an embroidery design for the jacket front band. The designs on the sample garment are 4" long and 5/8" wide. The sample garment has 4 sets of the design spaced down the front. Mark placement on the organza as shown *(fig. 1)* and place WSS beneath the fabric. Embroider the front band. Remove the WSS and press the strip *(fig. 1)*.
2. Select the embroidery design for the organdy insertion strip. The finished band will be 3"; the design covers 2-5/8" in the pictured jacket. With WSS beneath the fabric, embroider the organza strips for the jacket fronts and the jacket back. Remove the WSS and press the strips *(fig. 2)*.

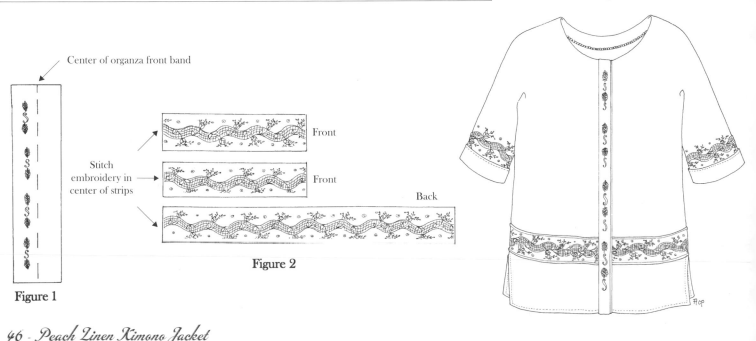

Center of organza front band

Stitch embroidery in center of strips

Front

Front

Back

Figure 2

Figure 1

Peach Linen Kimono Jacket

3. Position the embroidered lace insertion strips on the jacket fronts and the jacket back 6" from the bottom cut edge. Straight stitch the lace insertion strips in place 1/2" from the cut edge on both sides (**fig. 3**). Trim the lace insertion seam to 1/8". Stitch the lace insertion strip in place with an appliqué stitch covering the machine stitches and the raw edge of the organza (**fig. 4**).

4. Place the embroidered organza front band over the fabric band with the wrong side of the organza to the right side of the fabric (**fig. 5**). Fold the band in half with the organza right sides together. Stitch across the bottom and top edges of the band with a 5/8" seam. Trim and finish the seam (**fig. 6**). Turn the band with the right side out and press (**fig. 7**).

5. Refer to the Kimono Jacket general direction step 1.

6. Embroider each sleeve edge placing the lower edge of the embroidery 1" from the raw edge of the sleeve. Stitch the design across the front and back of the sleeve (**fig. 8**).

7. Refer to the Kimono Jacket general direction steps 2-4. Press the seam and facing away from the jacket.

8. Understitch the facing close to the neck seam (**fig. 9**). Finish the outer edge of the facing with an overcast or zigzag. Fold the facing to the wrong side of the jacket.

9. Refer to the Kimono Jacket general directions steps 7-9.

10. Place the embroidered front band with the right side of the band to the right side of the right jacket front. The band should meet the finished edges of the jacket front at the neck. Pin in place. Stitch 1/2" from the raw edge to attach the band to the jacket front (**fig. 10**).

11. Refer to the Kimono Jacket general direction steps 10-12.

12. Stitch the backside of the band in place by hand.

13. Mark buttonhole placement on the fabric band. Work buttonholes. Mark button placement and sew on buttons (**fig. 11**).

14. Press the embroidered front band toward the facing covering the buttonholes. Tack the embroidered front band to the jacket buttonhole band with a blind stitch in several places.

15. Refer to the Kimono Jacket general direction steps 15-17. The cuff will be left extended and not folded toward the sleeve.

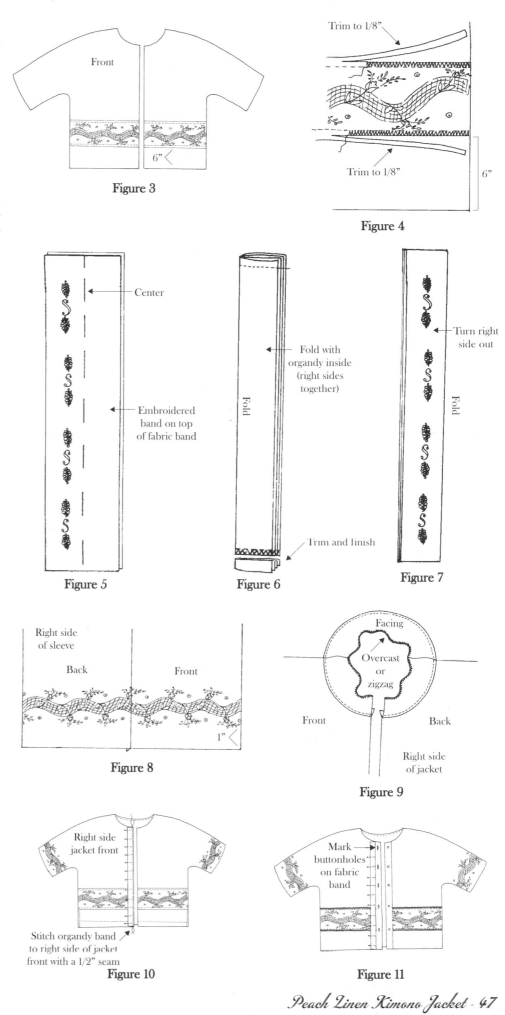

Figure 3

Figure 4

Figure 5

Figure 6

Figure 7

Figure 8

Figure 9

Figure 10

Figure 11

Peach Linen Kimono Jacket - 47

Heirloom Patchwork Linen Jacket

Connie Palmer, an educator for Husqvarna/Viking, made this fabulous blue linen jacket that is trimmed with many heirloom laces and stitches. Combining machine embroidery in ecru thread with ecru round thread laces was the grand plan for this jacket, and the patchwork techniques could not be more fascinating. The front pieces are made in blocks and feature double-needle pintucks, laces joined with machine bridging, machine embroidery, and folded tucks. The laces are stitched to the linen using wing-needle entredeux. A single row of gimp work is found at the top of the cuff and five beautiful pearl buttons close the front. The linen bias skirt is simple and fabulous to wear with this elegant jacket.

This suit would be at the head of the Easter parade in any city. I would also love this suit for a special occasion such as mother-of-the-bride or groom or for a graduation suit. Joanna had a white linen tailored suit for her high school graduation; this suit would be just as beautiful in white. Whatever the occasion, this suit is sure to please almost everybody who appreciates beautiful things.

- This jacket was made with reference to the Long Sleeve Jacket General Directions found on page 16.
- The skirt was made by the Bias Skirt General Directions found on page 10.

Note: The embroideries on this jacket are from Husqvarna Viking Embroidery Disks #32, #45 and #111 or you may choose other designs

Supplies

- Refer to the fabric requirements for the Long Sleeve Jacket adding 1 yard to the size you are making. BE SURE to read through entire instructions before purchasing fabric or cutting out the jacket.
- 11 yds of 5/8" ecru insertion
- Gimp cord

- DMC Perle cotton #12 ecru
- Sulky® thread #1082
- 60 wt. ecru cotton thread to match lace
- 80 wt. ecru Tanne thread to match lace
- Ultra Solvy™
- Tear-away stabilizer
- XS – MD = 1-3/8 yards interfacing or LG – 3XL = 1-3/4 yards interfacing
- Wash-out marker
- KK2000™
- 5 buttons (5/8")
- #90 universal needle
- #80 universal needle
- #110 universal needle
- 2.5/80 twin needle
- Open toe foot
- Edge stitching foot
- 5 groove pintuck foot
- Basic sewing supplies

Pattern Pieces

- Refer to the pattern pieces needed for the Long Sleeve Jacket General Directions, omitting the jacket pocket.

Cutting

- Cut one jacket back on the fold
- Cut two jacket sleeves
- Cut two jacket front band and facing and two from interfacing
- Cut one jacket back facing on the fold and one from interfacing
- Cut two jacket sleeve facing/cuffs and two from interfacing

Heirloom Patchwork Linen Jacket

—Directions—

Use the following designs or choose another embroidery design:

- Block #2 was embroidered using Husqvarna Viking Embroidery Disk # 45, Design #2 or you may choose an alternate design (design size = 6-1/4" by 3-3/4".)
- Block #4 was embroidered using Husqvarna Viking Embroidery Disk #45, Design #5 or you may choose an alternate design (design size = 3-1/4" by 6-1/4").
- Block #6 was embroidered using Husqvarna Viking Embroidery Disk # 111, Design #2:2. Mirror image side to side (design size = 5-1/4" by 8-1/4").
- Block #7 was embroidered using Husqvarna Viking Embroidery Disk #32, Design #28 (design size 7/8" by 1-1/4").

Make a tissue pattern for each block as follows:

1. Trace and cut out a tissue pattern of the right and left fronts of the jacket *(fig. 1)*.
2. Draw horizontal and vertical lines as shown in figure 1 (the lines with the X's). Mark the X's.
3. Label each block as designated #1 - #7.
4. Cut the blocks apart on the horizontal and vertical lines.
5. Place each tissue block onto another square of tissue. Trace a new pattern adding a 5/8" seam allowance on the X'ed sides only. Dot in the previous line which will now be the seam line *(fig. 2)*. Immediately discard the tissue piece without the seam allowance to avoid confusion.
6. Label and cut out each new block. You will have 6 pattern pieces with the seam allowances added *(fig. 3)*.

Creating the Lace Bands
(Eight yards of lace insertion has been allotted for the lace bands)

1. Wind Perle cotton on bobbin. You will use this bobbin on the top of the machine.
2. Use 60 wt. cotton in the bobbin.
3. Put a #90 universal needle in the machine.
4. Use an open-toe foot if available.
5. Cut 3 pieces of insertion 96" long.
6. Spray the wrong side of the lace strips with KK2000™ and place them on a piece of Ultra Solvy™, 1/4" apart.
7. Sew between the strips using a machine featherstitch adjusting the width so that the stitch catches the headings of the lace *(fig. 4)*. A featherstitch by hand may be used in place of a machine featherstitch.

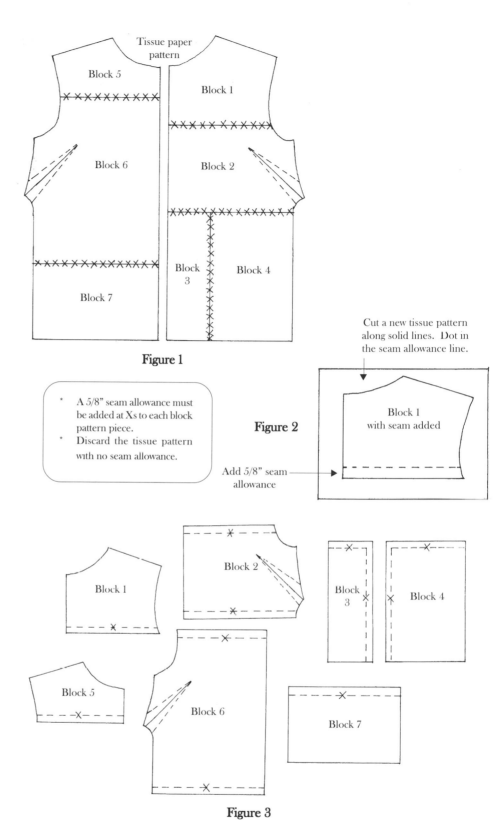

Figure 1

* A 5/8" seam allowance must be added at Xs to each block pattern piece.
* Discard the tissue pattern with no seam allowance.

Figure 2

Cut a new tissue pattern along solid lines. Dot in the seam allowance line.

Block 1 with seam added

Add 5/8" seam allowance

Figure 3

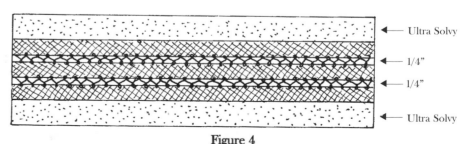

Figure 4

Ultra Solvy

1/4"

1/4"

Ultra Solvy

8. The lace band will be cut into smaller sections later.

9. All lace bands will be added to the fabric after the blocks are sewn together.

10. Rinse away the stabilizer and press the lace panels well.

Embellishment of pieces
BLOCK #1

(Three yards of lace insertion have been allotted for this block)

1. Cut a block of fabric 2" larger on all sides than your block #1 tissue pattern.

2. Trace diagonal lines 2" apart on the fabric with blue water soluble fabric pen creating a grid on the square of fabric *(fig. 5)*.

3. Center 5/8" insertion on lines and zigzag both sides of the insertion (L-1.5, W-1.5) *(fig. 6)*.

4. Once all the insertion is attached, pinstitch both sides of the insertion (L=2.5 W=2.0) with tear-away stabilizer underneath.

5. Lay the block #1 tissue pattern onto the embellished block #1 piece.

6. Trace the pattern onto the fabric. Cut only on the X'ed side where the seam allowance was added *(fig. 7)*. Lay the piece aside.

BLOCK #2

1. Cut a block of fabric 2" larger on all sides than your block #2 tissue pattern. Trace the pattern onto the fabric.

2. Refer to figure 8 for distance to be left between side of the embroidery and edges of block #2.

3. Trace the dart and all seam lines before embroidering. Hoop a square of stabilizer and adhere the fabric to the stabilizer placing your chosen embroidery design 2" from the top and 1" from the side of the drawn block. Do not sew the dart. Embroider the block and remove the stabilizer.

4. Lay the tissue pattern onto the block. If necessary, retrace the lines of block #2.

5. Cut only on the X'ed sides where the seam allowances were added *(fig. 9)*. Lay the piece aside.

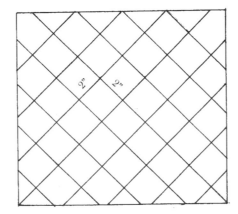

Figure 5

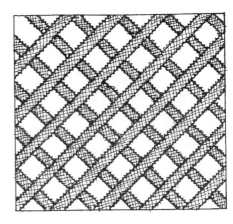

Figure 6

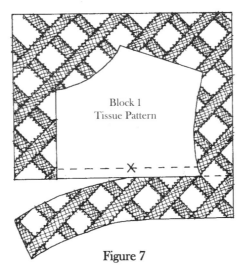

Figure 7

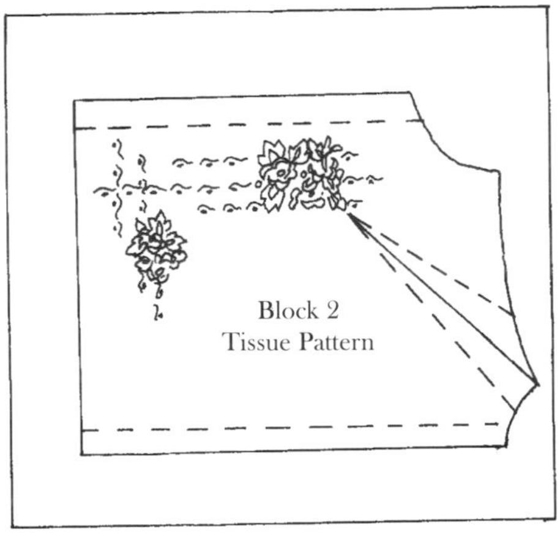

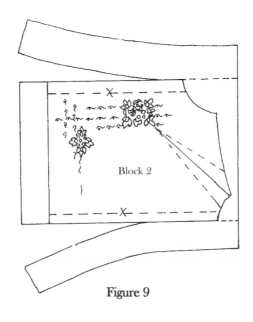

Figure 8

Figure 9

BLOCK #3

1. Cut a piece of fabric 2" wider and 7" longer than your block #3 tissue pattern.
2. Starting 2" from the top make a mark every 1-1/4". Pull a thread or draw a horizontal line on the first 8 marks *(fig. 10)*.
3. Fold each tuck wrong sides together on the pulled thread line. Stitch a tuck 1/4" from each fold line *(fig. 11)*.
4. Lay the tissue pattern on the block. Add additional tucks if necessary leaving the 1"hem allowance without tucks. There will be excess fabric at the bottom of the tucked strip.
5. When sufficient tucks are completed, Trace the block #3 pattern onto the tucked piece placing the top of the tissue pattern even with the top of the strip. Cut only on the X'ed sides where the seam allowances were added *(fig. 12)*. Lay the piece aside.

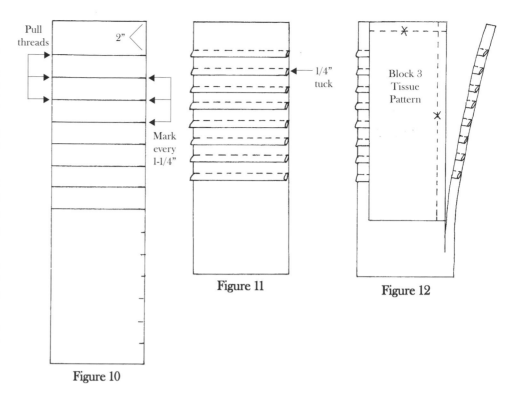

Figure 11

Figure 12

Figure 10

BLOCK #4

1. Cut a block of fabric 2" larger on all sides than your block #4 tissue pattern.
2. Fold the block into quarters and mark the center with a wash-out marker *(fig. 13)*
3. With stabilizer behind the fabric, complete the embroidery in the center of the block using the embroidery design listed above or a design of your choice.
4. When the embroidery is complete, remove the stabilizer and press the block well.
5. Lay the tissue pattern onto the block centering the embroidery design. Trace the pattern onto the embroidered piece marking the X'ed sides. Cut only on the X'ed sides where the seam allowances were added *(fig. 14)*. Lay the piece aside.

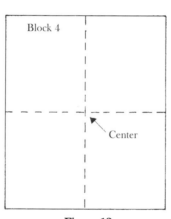

Figure 13

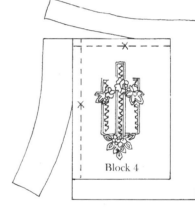

Figure 14

BLOCK #5

1. Cut a block of fabric 4" larger on all sides than your block #5 tissue pattern.
2. Trace a diagonal line on the block of fabric *(fig. 15)*.
3. Using a 5-groove pintuck foot and 2.5/80 twin needle stitch a tuck on the first pintuck line.
4. Sew all other tucks a foot's width away *(fig. 16)*.
5. Lay the tissue pattern onto the tucked block. Trace the pattern marking the X'ed side. Cut only on the X'ed side where the seam allowance was added *(fig. 17)*. Lay the piece aside.

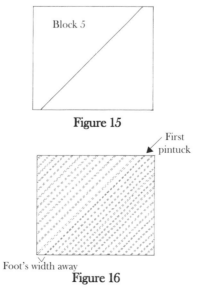

Figure 15

Figure 16

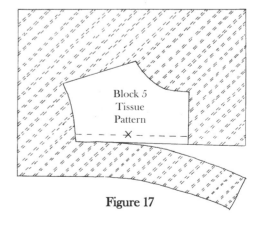

Figure 17

BLOCK #6

1. Cut a block of fabric 4" larger on all sides than your block #6 tissue pattern.
2. Center the tissue pattern over the block and trace the lines shown in figure 18 including the line for stippling.
3. Stipple a line of stipple stitching as shown in figure 19. If you are stipple stitching free-handed, refer to the technique for Stipple Stitching and create a line of stipple stitching no wider than 5/8" along the drawn line *(fig. 19)*. The stipple stitching on the jacket pictured was stitched using ecru Perle cotton in the bobbin (bypass tension) and ecru 60 wt. thread on the top. The stitching was done with the wrong side of the fabric up so the Perle cotton is visible on the right side of the fabric. Retrace pattern after stippling is complete.
4. The dart and large embroidery are not done at this time.
5. Lay the tissue pattern on the block. Cut the block only on the X'ed sides where the seam allowances were added *(fig. 20)*.

BLOCK #7

1. Cut a block of fabric 2" larger on all sides than your block #7 tissue pattern.
2. Trace the lines of the tissue pattern onto the block including the foldline for the 1" hem allowance and the seam allowances for the remaining three sides. Mark the seam allowance at the top with an X *(fig. 21)*.
3. Determine the embroidery placements on block #7 according to the size of the embroidery you chose. The embroidery on the pictured jacket measures 7/8" wide by 1-1/4" tall. Space the embroidery as shown in figure 22. This is only a representation since the measurements will vary according to the size garment you are making and the embroidery chosen. Adjust the distance between the design as needed. Do not extend the embroidery beyond the seam allowances or hem foldline.
4. Cut the block only on the X'ed side where the seam allowance was added *(fig. 23)*. Lay the piece aside.

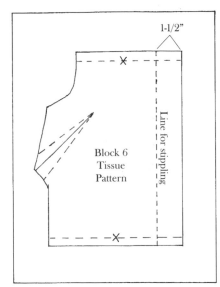

Figure 18

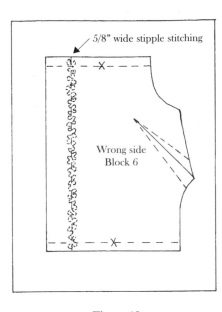

Figure 19

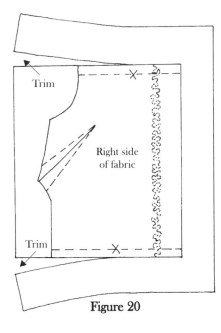

Figure 20

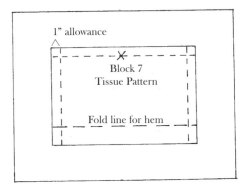

Figure 21

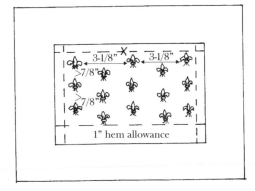

Figure 22

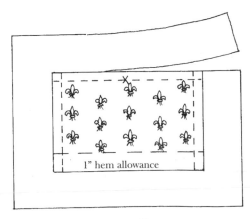

Figure 23

Construction

1. Place the blocks in the order shown in figure 24.
2. Matching the X'ed sides and pattern lines, stitch the blocks together in the order listed.
   a. Attach block 1 to block 2.
   b. Attach block 3 to the left side of block 4.
   c. Attach block 3/4 to the lower edge of block 2.
   d. Attach block 6 to the lower edge of block 5.
   e. Attach block #7 to the lower edge of block 6.
3. Trim all seam allowances to 1/4" and finish with a serge or overcast.
4. If necessary, re-trace the jacket fronts onto the panels adjusting as needed to balance the pieces. Cut out the jacket fronts *(fig. 25)*.
5. Sew the darts in the two jacket fronts.
6. Stabilize, hoop and complete the embroidery in the open space of block #6 allowing room for the lace panel to be added. You may use the embroidery design given above or use one of your choice within the dimensions of the design. Remove the stabilizer
7. Place the lace bands onto the panels allowing the ends of the lace bands to extent past the edges of the jacket. Sew the lace bands to the panels in the order indicated in figure 26 (some lace bands are over seams and some are not). Trim the top end of lace band #2 and both ends of lace band #4 where they will extend approximately 1/4" under the bands which overlap them. Pinstitch (L=2.5, W=2.0) or zigzag both sides of each band to attach them to the fabric. DO NOT trim fabric from behind lace. Baste the edges of the lace bands within the seam allowance of the jacket. Trim the excess away.
8. Refer to the Long Sleeve Jacket General Directions and complete steps 2 - 9.
9. Refer to the Long Sleeve Jacket General Directions and complete steps 14 - 20.
10. On the side of the cuff which will show when turned up, stitch a satin stitch over gimp cord a foot's width away from the edge of the cuff *(fig. 27)*.
11. Refer to the Long Sleeve Jacket General Directions and complete steps 21 - 23.

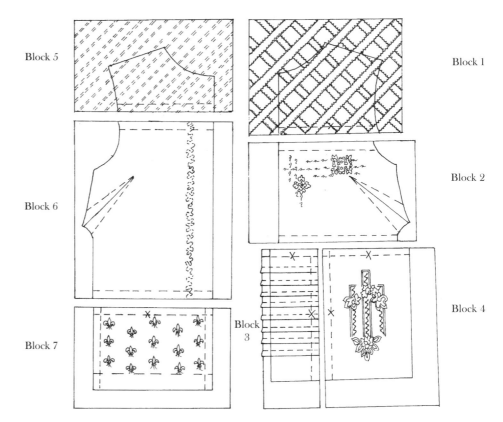

Figure 24

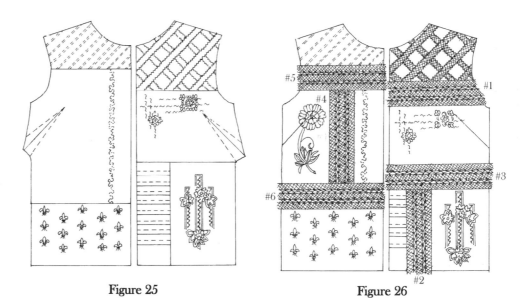

Figure 25   **Figure 26**

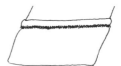

Figure 27

Black & Blue Color-Blocked Jacket

This jacket, made by Joyce Drexler of Sulky® of America, features black and blue silk blocked in a most unusual way, using the long sleeve; jacket pattern in this book. The color-blocked front and back are designed on tissue paper. The pockets and cuffs are black. The embroidery design is from "Inspirational Concept" by Amazing Designs®. The design is stitched three times and placed on the jacket to create a continuous floral design that is really very large. Sulky Puffy Foam™ used underneath the machine embroidery gives a raised look to the embroidery. Very unusual buttons are used to close the front of the jacket.

- This jacket was made with reference to the Long Sleeve Jacket General Directions found on page 16.

Note: The embroidery on the jacket front is from The Embroidery Card AD-3000 "Inspirational Concept" from Amazing Designs®. The design is stitched three times and then placed on the jacket to create a continuous floral design.

Supplies

- Refer to the Long Sleeve Jacket General Directions for the fabric requirements (The amount given will be for the blue on the jacket)
- 2-1/2 yards of a contrasting fabric (black on the sample garment)

- Thread to match both fabrics
- XS – MD = 1-3/8 yards interfacing
- LG – 4XL = 1-3/4 yards interfacing
- Three squares of Sulky Soft 'n Sheer™ stabilizer to fit your machine hoop
- Sulky thread for your chosen embroidery design to complement your fabrics
- Squares of Sulky Puffy Foam™ to blend with your chosen Sulky colors onto which the embroidery design will be stitched
- 4 buttons (5/8")
- Amazing Designs® Embroidery Card AD-3000 "Inspirational Concept" or another embroidery design of your choice
- Basic sewing supplies

Pattern Pieces

Refer to the Long Sleeve Jacket Directions for the pattern pieces needed

* All seams are 5/8" unless otherwise noted. To finish seam, trim seam to 1/4" and overcast edge by machine or serger.

—Directions—

Making Free-Form Appliqué Motifs

Refer to the technique for Free-Form Machine Appliqué, steps 1 – 4, and complete three of the floral motifs using the embroidery card listed above or you may use another embroidery of your choice. Set the motifs aside.

Making a Patchwork Pattern

1. Cut two tissue patterns from the jacket front pattern for the left and right jacket front.
2. Place the tissue patterns on a flat surface with the front edges together.
3. Using a yardstick, draw lines onto the tissue pattern in the approximate placement as shown (fig. 1).
4. On the straight lines drawn with the yard stick make a notation to add seam allowances to each side.
5. Label the pieces as shown (fig. 1), putting piece number and color on each tissue piece.
6. Mark the grain line on each piece (fig. 1).

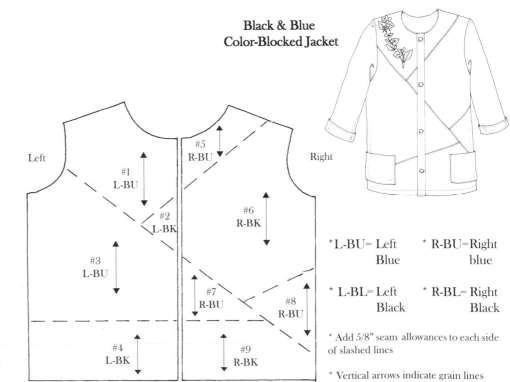

Black & Blue Color-Blocked Jacket

Left   Right

#1 L-BU
#2 L-BK
#3 L-BU
#4 L-BK
#5 R-BU
#6 R-BK
#7 R-BU
#8 R-BU
#9 R-BK

*L-BU= Left Blue   * R-BU=Right blue

* L-BL= Left Black   * R-BL= Right Black

* Add 5/8" seam allowances to each side of slashed lines

* Vertical arrows indicate grain lines

Figure 1

Cutting the Patchwork Pieces

1. Cut the tissue pieces apart along the straight lines *(fig. 2)*.
2. Place each tissue piece on the designated fabric color. Draw around the outside jacket shape of the tissue piece (not along the edge to which seam allowances must be added).
3. Along the line to which seam allowances need to be added, dot in a stitching line. Draw a straight line 5/8" from the dotted line. The straight line will be your cutting line *(fig. 3)*.
4. Cut out the pieces along the cutting lines.
5. Be sure to keep the pieces labeled so that you will be able to put them together in the right order.

Building the Front Panels

1. Attach the pieces to each other in the order listed below. Follow steps 2 – 3 for stitching instructions.
   a. Attach #1 to #2.
   b. Attach #1/#2 to #3.
   c. Attach #3 to #4.
   d. Attach #5 to #6.
   e. Attach #6 to #8.
   f. Attach #7 to #9.
   g. Attach #6/#8 to #7/#9.
2. Pin the fabric pieces together and stitch with a 5/8" seam allowance (refer to figure 2 for placement).
3. Press the seam allowances open. Finish each seam allowance separately.
4. Topstitch 1/4" on each side of the seam using thread to match the fabric on which you are stitching.
5. Press the pieces well *(fig. 4)*.

Cutting the Pieces

- Cut one jacket back on the fold from the blue fabric
- Cut two jacket sleeves from the blue fabric
- Cut one jacket back facing on the fold from the blue fabric and one from interfacing
- Cut two jacket pockets from the black fabric
- Cut two front bands and facings from the black fabric and two from interfacing.
- Cut two sleeve cuffs from the black fabric and two from interfacing

Construction

1. Position the three motifs on the jacket front referring to the finished drawing.
2. Refer to the technique Free-Form Appliqué, steps 5 – 6, and attach the motifs to the jacket front.
3. Refer to the Long Sleeve Jacket General Directions, steps 1 – 23 and complete the jacket. Four buttonholes and buttons are placed equal distance apart along the front placket.

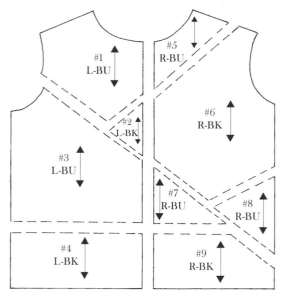

* Add 5/8" seam allowances to each side of slashed lines

* Vertical arrows indicate grain lines

Figure 2

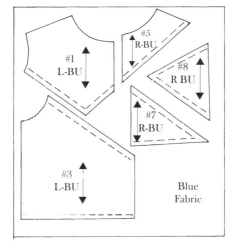

Figure 3

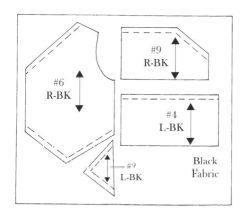

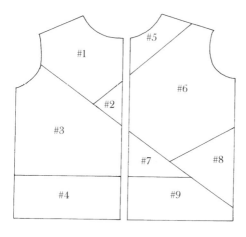

Figure 4

Color-Blocked Silk Jacket

What a wonderful jacket made in three different colors of silk. Carol Ingram of Sulky of America designed it. Two shades of teal and one shade of lime green make a fabulous combination for this super fun jacket. Machine-embroidered shoes in black, gray and gold are featured on the grid work pockets as well as on the upper left-hand corner of the jacket. Wonderful buttons in black and gold are used to close the jacket.

The grid work pockets are made of tulle (or netting) and gimp cord using a machine satin stitch to make the grid. The embroidery card is a Cactus Punch® Signature card. Sulky Puffy Foam™ is used for the shoe embroidery and it makes the shoes a little bit three-dimensional. This jacket will also be featured in Sulky Secrets to Successful Appliqué, Book 14.

- This jacket was made with reference to the Long Sleeve Jacket General Directions found on page 16.
- This jacket was embroidered using the Catus Punch™ Signature Series #61 "Steppin' Out" embroidery card.

Supplies

- 2 yards of light teal fabric for back, one sleeve, and color blocks on front
- 1-2/3 yards of medium teal fabric for color blocks on the front and one sleeve
- 1-1/8 yards of lime fabric for front band, back facing, and cuffs
  The colors above will be referred to in the directions below. You may substitute other colors as desired.

- XS – MD = 1-3/8 yards interfacing
- LG – 4XL = 1-3/4 yards interfacing
- 7 buttons (5/8")
- Thread to match fabrics
- Cording or piping foot
- Sulky Ultra Solvy™
- Temporary spray adhesive
- Tulle or netting - two pieces 12" by 14" for the pockets
- Three squares of tulle or netting large enough to fit your hoop and embroider your chosen design
- Fine-line, permanent-ink black marker
- Ruler with a 45-degree angle
- Gimp cord
- Decorative threads (for embroidery, appliqué or other creative stitching)
- Black decorative thread

- Sulky Soft'n Sheer™ stabilizer
- Sulky 2mm Puffy Foam™ color to closely match design threads (3 squares larger than your chosen design)
- Wood burning tool or stencil cutter
- Polyester invisible thread
- Thread to match fabric

Pattern Pieces

- Long Sleeve Jacket Front
- Long Sleeve Jacket Back
- Long Sleeve Jacket Dleeve
- Long Sleeve Jacket Front Band and Facing
- Long Sleeve Jacket Back Facing
- Long Sleeve Jacket Sleeve Facing/Cuff

Color-Blocked Silk Jacket

Creating the Color Block Front and Cutting the Pieces

1. Cut a tissue block 2" larger on all sides than the jacket front you are making *(fig. 1)*.
2. Draw a line across the block 1/3 of the distance from the top, dividing the tissue block into the proportions shown in *figure 2*.
3. Cut the tissue pattern apart on the drawn line *(fig. 3)*.
4. From the smaller rectangle, cut two light teal blocks. Lay the pieces aside.
5. From the larger rectangle, cut two medium teal blocks. Lay the pieces aside.
6. Position the pieces as shown in *figure 4*.
7. Stitch the colors together with a 1/2" seam, placing them right sides together. Finish the seam *(fig. 5)*. Press the seam towards the darker color.
8. Place the two created color block panels right sides together *(fig. 6a)* and cut the two jacket fronts from the panels. Mark the darts *(fig. 6b)*.
9. Cut one sleeve from the light teal fabric.
10. Cut one jacket back on the fold from the light teal fabric.
11. Cut one sleeve from the dark teal fabric.
12. From the lime fabric and interfacing, cut the following:
    - Two jacket front band and facings
    - One jacket back facing on the fold
    - Two jacket sleeve facing cuffs

* All seams are 5/8" unless otherwise noted. To finish seam, trim seam to 1/4" and overcast edge by machine or serger.

—Directions—

To create the pocket:

1. Cut a piece of Ultra Solvy™ and black netting 12" by 14" for each pocket.
2. Using a fine-line, permanent-ink, black marker and a ruler, draw a 6" by 8" pocket shape onto the Ultra Solvy™. Round off the bottom corners *(fig. 7)*.
3. Use a ruler with a 45-degree angle and the fine-line, permanent-ink marker to draw diagonal lines approximately 1" apart across the drawn pattern in both directions *(fig. 8)*.
4. Using Sulky KK 2000™, lightly spray the Ultra Solvy™ and lay the tulle or netting over it.
5. Thread the top and bobbin with black decorative thread and attach a cording or piping foot to the machine.

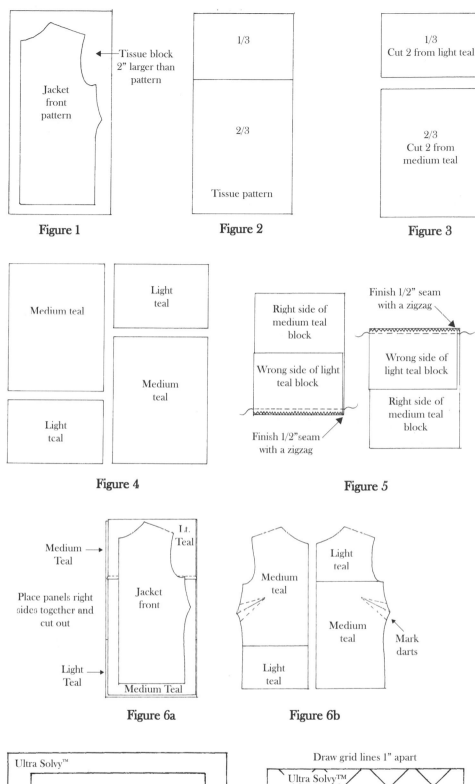

Figure 1

Figure 2

Figure 3

Figure 4

Figure 5

Figure 6a

Figure 6b

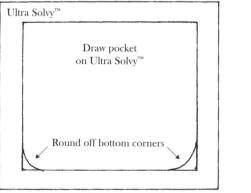

Figure 7

Figure 8

6. Lay the gimp cord or other heavyweight cord over one of the drawn lines and sew a 3mm wide satin stitch over it. Leave approximately 1/2" of gimp extending beyond the end of each row, to be clipped off later *(fig. 9)*. Satin stitch over cord on all lines, in both directions.

7. Clip off all extended tails. Lay the cord around the outside of the sewn grid and satin stitch over it, catching and covering the clipped ends of each row as you stitch. Stitch completely around the grid *(fig. 10)*. Increase your satin stitch to 4mm and go around the outside of the grid once again to secure the ends.

8. Cut away tulle or netting from around the outside edges of the grid.

9. Trim away excess Ultra Solvy™ from around the grid pocket and place the pocket in tepid water, covering it completely. Soak 5 to 10 minutes to completely dissolve the Ultra Solvy™. Rinse thoroughly. Blot dry with a towel and lay aside to dry completely.

10. Apply any computerized machine embroidery design onto the grid (refer to the technique Free-Form Machine Appliqué). Three designs will be needed, one for each pocket and one for the upper left front. Refer to the finished drawing.

11. Iron Totally Stable™ onto the reverse side of the garment where the pocket will be placed; if the fabric is thin or flimsy, use two layers of Totally Stable™.

12. When the "Grid Pocket" is dry, spray KK 2000™ on the wrong side of the grid and temporarily adhere it onto the garment. Use the placement line for the top of the pocket on the pattern as a guide for placement of the pocket. Use black decorative thread or dark invisible thread and a short, narrow zigzag stitch to stitch around the outside of the pocket, leaving open at the top.

Construction of Jacket

1. Refer to Long Sleeve Jacket steps 1-9.
2. Refer to Long Sleeve Jacket steps 14-17.
3. Refer to Long Sleeve Jacket steps 18-23.
4. Attach the third free form design to the upper left jacket front. Refer to the technique Free Form Applique.

**Detail of
Color-Blocked Silk Jacket**

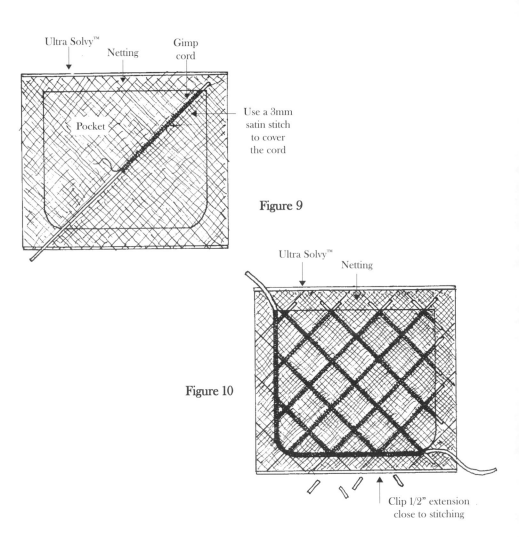

Figure 9

Figure 10

Clip 1/2" extension close to stitching

Cream Linen Jacket with Bobbin Work

What could be more elegant than a cream, linen-blend suit with trim on the pockets and cuffs? Coni Martin of Janome designed this tailored but spiffy ensemble. The basic long-sleeved jacket is completely plain except for the reverse bobbin work stitched in several types of blue decorative threads on the pockets and sleeves. The threads include silk ribbon, floss, and a thread with silver woven through it. All in all, this jacket is sure to bring rave reviews. The front is left unbuttoned. The tank and pointed-gore skirt are also made from the same fabric. This jacket is the perfect palette for embellishment of any type, but this pocket/cuff trim is most striking.

- This jacket was made with reference to the Long Sleeve Jacket General Directions found on page 16.
- The skirt was made by the Gore Skirt General Directions found on page 12.
- The tank was made by the Tank General Directions, Lined Version found on page 5.

- The couching of the decorative cords was done on a Janome sewing machine using the Miracle Stitcher™.

Supplies

- Refer to the fabric yardage and notions needed in the Long Sleeve Jacket General Directions, omitting the seven 5/8" buttons.
- 4mm silk ribbon and plastic canvas metallic yarn were used for this jacket. You will need several yards of each.
- Basic sewing supplies.

Pattern Pieces

- Refer to the Long Sleeve Jacket General Directions

Cutting the Pieces

- Refer to the Long Sleeve Jacket General Directions

* All seams are 5/8" unless otherwise noted. To finish seam, trim seam to 1/4" and overcast edge by machine or serger.

—Directions—

1. Wind the decorative thread on the bobbin by placing the bobbin on the bobbin winder and holding the decorative thread in your hand or let it reel off a pencil held in front of the bobbin winder.
2. Wind at an even speed guiding the thread with your fingers.
3. Thread the top of the machine with regular sewing thread in a color that matches the background of your fabric.
4. Place the bobbin into the machine bypassing the bobbin tension. Turn the hand wheel to bring the decorative bobbin thread up. It will not be in any tension guide in the bobbin area. Select a decorative stitch that is not very dense and travels in a long forward motion. Experiment on fabric scraps before stitching on your project, adjusting the top tension as necessary to achieve the look you want.
5. Starch two of the pockets and the two cuffs. Place the fabric WRONG SIDE up and stitch the decorative stitching in a random pattern onto two pockets and the two cuffs. The decorative stitching on the cuffs will need to be between the fold line and the seam allowance which will attach to the lower edge of the sleeve. Avoid stitching decorative threads in the seam allowances of the cuffs or the pockets **(fig. 1)**.
6. Refer to the Long Sleeve Jacket General Directions steps 1 – 20 and step 23. The jacket was made without buttons to be an open front jacket.

**Cream Linen Jacket
with Bobbin Work**

Figure 1

Pink Linen Arizona Jacket

Created by June Mellinger of Brother, this suit reminds me of Arizona. Made of a dusty medium pink linen, the suit has pretty machine zigzag-type embroidery trims that lend a southwestern influence. The machine stitching, in a shade of darker pink, is found on both sides of the front plackets, across the top of the pockets, and around the cuffs. The short sleeve shell top, made in a matching fabric, has decorative stitching around the neckline; the hems on both the sleeves and the bottom are stitched with wing-needle entredeux. The matching bias skirt has decorative stitching around the hemline.

- This jacket was made with reference to the Long Sleeve Jacket General Directions found on page 16.
- The shell was made by the Shell General Directions – Short Sleeve Version found on page 6, adding decorative stitching around the neck, hemline and sleeves.
- The skirt was made by the Bias Skirt General Directions found on page 10, adding the embroidery to match the jacket on the front waistband and decorative stitching at the hemline.

Note: The embroidery on this jacket is made up of a satin-stitched zigzag pattern with a narrow decorative stitch just above the satin stitch following the same line of the zigzag shape. Machine-stitched eyelet circles are centered above each V of the zigzag shape.

* All seams are 5/8" unless otherwise noted. To finish seam, trim seam to 1/4" and overcast edge by machine or serger.

Supplies

- Refer to the fabric yardage and notions for the Long Sleeve Jacket, omitting the buttons
- Sewing thread to match fabric
- Machine embroidery thread which will complement fabric
- Tear-away stabilizer
- #80 universal machine needle
- Basic sewing supplies

Pattern Pieces

- Refer to the pattern pieces needed for the Long Sleeve Jacket General Directions
- Arizona Jacket Embroidery Template

Cutting the Pieces

- Refer to the layout and the cutting directions in the Long Sleeve Jacket General Directions

—Directions—

1. Trace the seam line and the fold line on the right side of the two front facing pieces. Trace the template onto the front band (**fig. 1**).
2. Place tear-away stabilizer beneath the front facing and machine embroider the design centered between the two lines. Remove the stabilizer and press well.
3. Place tear-away stabilizer beneath the top edge of the cuffs and the top edge of two of the pockets. Complete the embroidery approximately 1-1/4" below the cut edge. This will leave room for the 5/8" seam allowance with the embroidery placed below. Remove the stabilizer and press the pieces well (**fig. 2**).
4. Refer to Long Sleeve Jacket General Directions, steps 1 – 20 and step 23 to complete the jacket. This jacket does not button down the front.

Pink Linen Arizona Jacket

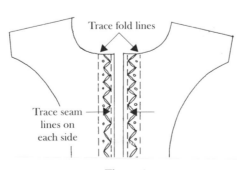

Trace fold lines

Trace seam lines on each side

Figure 1

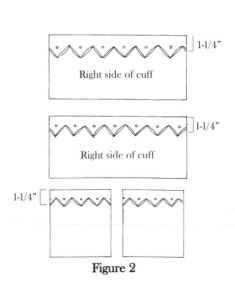

1-1/4"

Right side of cuff

1-1/4"

Right side of cuff

1-1/4"

Figure 2

Yellow Silk Ribbon Embroidered Jacket

Using some of my favorite colors, this jacket is made from a yellow rayon nubby fabric. Silk ribbon embroidery is stitched by hand down the front of the jacket in between the buttonholes. Beautiful decorative gold buttons finish the front treatment. This silk ribbon embroidery is also found on the pockets. An interesting pocket feature is the use of a buttonhole and button to close the center top of the pocket. The silk ribbon embroidery is worked in earth-tone shades of gray, green, yellow and tan. Both the tank and pointed gore skirt are made of a beautiful rayon chiffon print which was the inspiration for the colors used in the silk ribbon embroidery on the jacket.

- This jacket was made with reference to the Long Sleeve Jacket General Directions found on page 16.
- The skirt was made by the Gore Skirt General Directions found on page 12.
- The tank was made by the Tank General Directions – Lined Version found on page 5.

Supplies

- Refer to the fabric yardage and notions for the Long Sleeve Jacket; jacket requires *six* buttons
- YLI Silk ribbon
  4mm Blue Gray #100
  4mm Gray Green #32
  4mm Yellow #14
  2mm Beige #34
- Sewing thread to match the fabric
- Six 5/8" buttons
- Basic sewing supplies

Pattern Pieces

- Refer to the pattern pieces needed for the Long Sleeve Jacket General Directions
- Embroidery Template for front facing
- Embroidery Template for pockets

Cutting the Pieces

- Refer to the layout for the Long Sleeve Jacket

* All seams are 5/8" unless otherwise noted. To finish seam, trim seam to 1/4" and overcast edge by machine or serger.

—Directions—

1. Trace embroidery designs onto the right front facing between the buttonhole markings and to the top of two of the pocket pieces *(fig. 1)*. Note: Four buttonholes are placed approximately 5" apart with embroidery in between.
2. Refer to the embroidery techniques and embroider the designs according to the template.
3. Refer to the Long Sleeve Jacket General Directions and complete steps 1-11. In step 10, be sure to leave the right edge open on one pocket, and the left edge on the other pocket.
4. Place a buttonhole in the top center of each pocket starting the buttonhole 5/8" from the top edge *(fig. 2)*.
5. Refer to the Long Sleeve Jacket General Directions and complete steps 12-23.

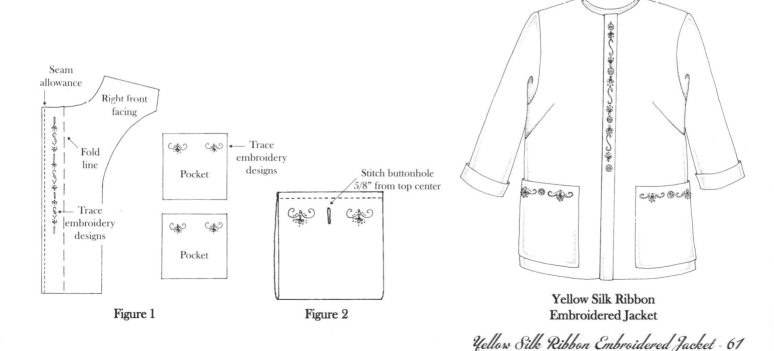

Seam allowance
Right front facing
Fold line
Trace embroidery designs

Pocket
Pocket
Trace embroidery designs

Stitch buttonhole 5/8" from top center

Figure 1

Figure 2

Yellow Silk Ribbon Embroidered Jacket

Reverse Embroidery & Couching Jacket

Using the basic long sleeve jacket pattern, this classic purple silk has hand-dyed, multi-colored silk along the bottom as well as on the cuffs of the sleeves. Presented by Sue Hausmann, Senior Vice President of Husqvarna/Viking, this jacket features decorative machine embroidery in v's, made using a mega-hoop borders disc. One could certainly get the look using a zigzag stitch in a "v" pattern if an embroidery unit is not available. Little green threads are couched in place to hang down at various places along the decorative stitching. Beautiful silver buttons were used to close the front of the jacket. The skirt made to match this jacket is the gore skirt with points. This suit was made for Sue Hausmann by Patti Jo Larson, an educator for Husqvarna/Viking.

- This jacket was made with reference to the Long Sleeve Jacket General Directions found on page 16.
- The skirt was made by the Gore Skirt General Directions found on page 12.

- The jacket embroidery used the Husqvarna Viking Mega Borders Disk 117 Design #10 to join the two fabrics. The eyelash yarn was couched. It took five mega hoopings to go around the jacket with border.

Supplies

- Refer to the fabric yardage for the Long Sleeve Jacket General Directions for the solid fabric – the jacket pictured was made to coordinate with the Color Blocked Long Sleeve Shell and Skirt. The cuffs and lower portion of the jacket are multi-colored and the upper portion and sleeves are a solid color.
- 7/8 yard of multi-colored fabric for the cuffs and lower portion of the jacket
- 2-1/2 yards of eyelash yarn to coordinate
- Decorative machine embroidery thread to coordinate
- #80 universal needle
- 1 yard of Sulky Totally Stable™ or tear-away stabilizer
- Thread to match fabric
- XS – MD = 1-3/8 yards of interfacing
- LG – 4XL = 1-3/4 yards of interfacing
- 7 buttons (5/8")
- Basic sewing supplies

Pattern pieces

- Refer to the pattern pieces listed in the Long Sleeve Jacket General Directions omitting the jacket pocket
- Optional: Border template for jacket

Cutting the Pieces

- Cut two jacket fronts from the solid fabric
- Cut one jacket back on the fold from the solid fabric
- Cut two jacket sleeves from the solid fabric
- Cut two jacket front band and facings and two from interfacing from the solid fabric
- Cut one jacket back facing on the fold and one from interfacing from the solid fabric
- Cut two jacket sleeve facing/cuffs from the multi-colored fabric and two from interfacing
- Draw a horizontal line 12" from the bottom edge of the pattern on both the jacket front and the jacket back. Cut a 12" band of the multi-colored fabric along the cutting lines of the jacket (two for the front and one on the fold for the back).

* All seams are 5/8" unless otherwise noted. To finish seam, trim seam to 1/4" and overcast edge by machine or serger.

Reverse Embroidery and Couching Jacket

—Directions—

1. Refer to the Long Sleeve Jacket General Directions and complete steps 1, 2, 9 and step 14. Finish the seams *(fig. 1)*.
2. Stitch the side seams of the 12" band and finish the seams *(fig. 2)*. Measure 10-1/2" from the bottom edge of the band and draw a horizontal line across the band.
3. Place the multi-colored band along the bottom edge of the jacket aligning the side seams. Adhere the band to the lower portion of the jacket with KK2000 *(fig. 3)*. The wrong side of the band will be to the right side of the jacket.
4. Adhere a 3" band of Totally Stable™ or tear-away stabilizer behind the main jacket fabric at the top edge of the 12" band.
5. The pictured jacket was made on a Viking Designer I using the Mega Hoop (Mega Borders disk 117 design #10) as follows:
   a. Use the Mega Hoop template to mark the placement of the Mega Border repeats.
   b. Hoop and forward stitch to sew the first zigzag outline. Stop.
   c. Slide off hoop and trim excess multi-colored fabric above the design from the topside of the jacket. Trim very close to the stitching.
   d. Slide the hoop back on and stitch the complete embroidery.
   e. Re-hoop and continue to complete the embroidered border.
   f. Remove from the hoop.
   g. From the inside of the jacket, trim away the solid jacket fabric from below the embroidered design.

6. To use the optional design template given omit step 5 above and stitch as follows:
   a. Transfer the design to the top layer of fabric centering the template on the drawn line on the band *(fig. 4)*.
   b. Stitch a small zigzag (L=1.0, W=2.0) along the template line *(fig. 4)*.
   c. Trim away the multi-colored fabric from above the design on the front side of the jacket *(fig. 5)*.
   d. Trim away the solid colored fabric from below the design on the inside of the jacket *(fig. 6)*.
   e. Stabilize and satin stitch (L=0.5, W=2.5) over the zigzag to complete the decorative stitching. Any additional satin stitched embellishment is done at this time.
7. Attach the eyelash yarn along the lower edge of the satin stitching around the border of the jacket using a couching stitch or a small zigzag *(fig. 7)*.
8. Refer to the Long Sleeve Jacket General Directions and complete steps 3 – 8.
9. The edge of the facing will be tacked to the seam allowance of the sleeve.
10. Refer to the Long Sleeve Jacket General Directions and complete steps 15 – 23.

> Figures 4-7 show optional border template design

Figure 1

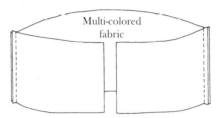

Multi-colored fabric

Figure 2

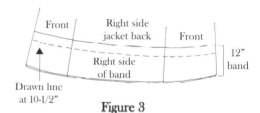

Front | Right side jacket back | Front
Right side of band | 12" band
Drawn line at 10-1/2"

Figure 3

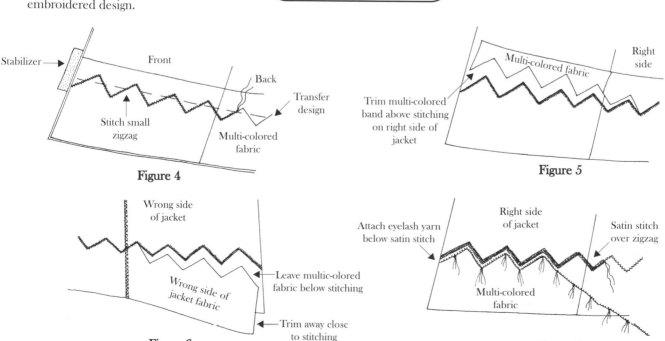

Stabilizer — Front — Back
Stitch small zigzag
Transfer design
Multi-colored fabric

Figure 4

Multi-colored fabric — Right side
Trim multi-colored band above stitching on right side of jacket

Figure 5

Wrong side of jacket
Wrong side of jacket fabric
Leave multi-colored fabric below stitching
Trim away close to stitching

Figure 6

Right side of jacket
Attach eyelash yarn below satin stitch
Satin stitch over zigzag
Multi-colored fabric

Figure 7

Color-Blocked Long Sleeve Shell

Using color-blocked panels, this blouse features purple, green, mauve and hand-dyed, multi-colored silk. Presented by Sue Hausmann, Senior Vice President of Husqvarna/Viking, the techniques are tailored and very interesting. For the center panel, variegated decorative thread is placed in the bobbin and interesting stitches are stitched from the back of the fabric; some people call this bobbin work. The color-block sections are stitched together, then decorative threads are couched over the seams. Couching is also used around the neckline. Some machines have feet made specifically for couching; some people like to use a pintuck foot to hold down the threads. The bias skirt made of the hand-dyed, multi-colored silk complements this wonderfully embellished blouse. This skirt and long-sleeved shell are very flattering to all figure types; it is also a very comfortable outfit. Patti Jo Larson, an educator for Husqvarna/Viking, made this outfit for Sue Hausmann.

- This shell was made with reference to the Shell General Directions, long sleeve, round neck version found on page 6.
- The skirt was made by the Bias Skirt General Directions found of page 10.
- Read through entire directions before purchasing fabric or cutting out the shell.

Supplies

- Refer to the fabric yardage in the Shell General Directions for the plum fabric
- 1/2 yard green fabric
- 1/2 yard mauve fabric
- 1/2 yard multi-colored fabric
- #80 universal needle
- Decorative thread (we used hand dyed #3 perle cotton in variegated colors to coordinate with the fabric choices)
- Sewing thread to match the fabric colors
- Invisible thread
- 5 or 7-hole cording foot
- Basic sewing supplies

Pattern Pieces

- Shell Front With Dart – Round Neck Version
- Shell Back
- Shell Long Sleeve

Cutting the Pieces

- Cut two sleeves from the plum fabric
- Cut one back on the fold from the plum fabric
- Cut one plum rectangle 15" by 36", cut two green rectangles 13-1/2" by 15", cut one mauve rectangle 13-1/2" by 9-1/4", cut one multi-colored rectangle 12" by 36". Refer to the directions, steps 1 -2 to create a panel for the shell front.
- Trace the shell front onto the fabric panel created for the front making sure that you balance and center the blocks of fabrics. Mark the darts.

—Directions—

1. Place the rectangles cut in the order shown *(fig. 1)*.
2. Stitch the pieces together with a 5/8" seam. Attach the three center rectangles first, then attach the top and bottom rectangles. Trim and finish the seam *(fig. 2)*. Press the panel well
3. Slowly wind decorative thread onto a bobbin. Place the bobbin into the machine and run the decorative thread through the bypass. Use thread to match the fabric or invisible thread in the top of the machine. Turn the hand wheel to bring the decorative thread to the surface of the machine.
4. You may want to test stitches on scrap fabric before decorative stitching onto the garment.
5. Hoop the fabric with the wrong side of the fabric facing up. On the Viking Designer I select Stitch E 24 (or the built-in stippling stitch) (L=6.0, W=15.0) and use the S foot. On other machines choose the stippling stitch or a forward motion stitch which is not dense.

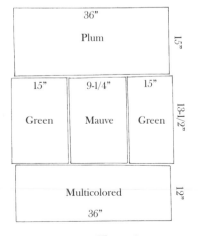

Figure 1

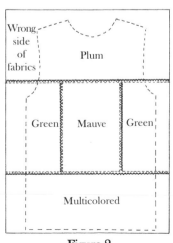

Figure 2

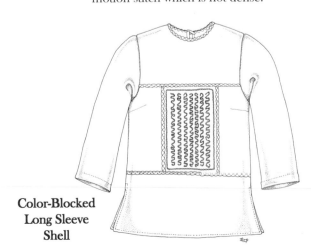

Color-Blocked Long Sleeve Shell

6. With the wrong side of the fabric up, stitch rows of stippling stitch to fill the center of the middle block on the shell front (*fig. 3a* shows wrong side, *fig. 3b* shows right side). Refer to the technique for Stipple Stitching. Leave tails of decorative thread at the beginning and end of each row. Straight stitch approximately 1/2" from the seam line around the stippling to "frame" the stitching. Take all tails of the decorative threads to the back with a needle just large enough to thread with the decorative thread. On the wrong side of the fabric, tie the tail of the decorative thread into a knot with the matching sewing thread to secure (*fig. 4*).

7. Place thread to match the fabric in the bobbin, threading the bobbin as for regular sewing. Place invisible thread in the top of the machine.

8. Run 5 – 7 lengths of the decorative thread into the holes of the cording foot allowing approximately 2" to extend in front of the foot. Choose a serpentine stitch adjusting the width of the stitch so that all decorative threads are caught in the stitching (*fig. 5*).

9. Stitch the decorative threads to the right side of the rectangle using the serpentine stitch beginning with the vertical seams of the front rectangle.

10. Stitch the decorative threads to the right side of the rectangle using the serpentine stitch along the horizontal seams of the front rectangle. On the horizontal seam lines, stitch the threads just beyond the drawn shell front.

11. Cut out the front shell from the created rectangles (*fig. 6*).

12. To make the placket in the back:
    a. Cut a 4" slit down the center back from the neck edge (*fig. 7*).
    b. Overcast the edge of the cut fabric (*fig. 8*).
    c. Beginning at the neck edge press 1/4" to the wrong side narrowing to 0" at the point of the V (*fig. 9*).
    d. Straight stitch the pressed under edge to secure (*fig. 9*).
    e. Referring to the directions above, stitch 5-7 decorative threads in place with a serpentine stitch along the finished edge of the slit (*fig. 10*).

13. Serge or overcast the raw edge of the fabric at the shoulders on both front shoulders and both back shoulders. Place the front shell to the back shell at the shoulders, right sides together and stitch. Press the seam open.

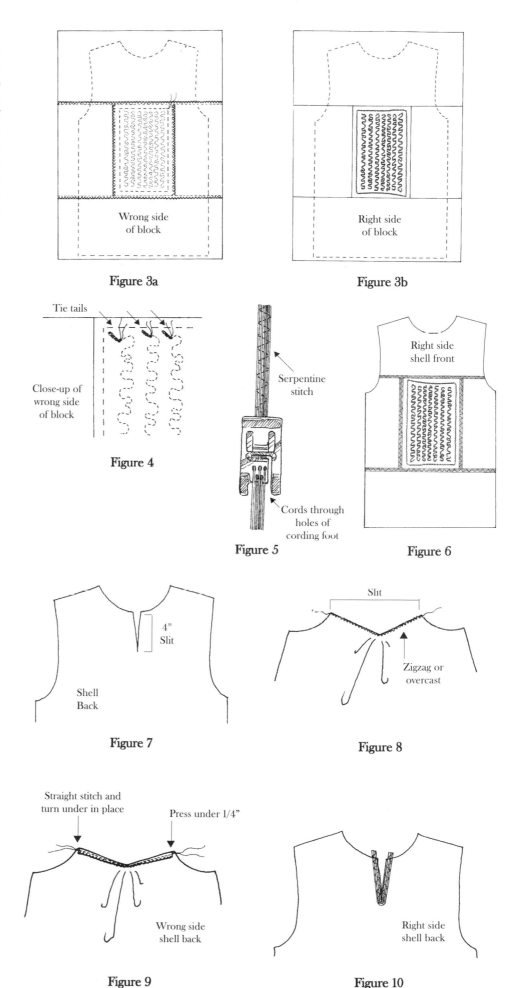

Figure 3a

Figure 3b

Figure 4

Figure 5

Figure 6

Figure 7

Figure 8

Figure 9

Figure 10

Color-Blocked Long Sleeve Shell - 65

14. Stay-stitch (short straight stitch) 5/8" from the raw edge of the neckline *(fig. 11-#1)*. Trim 3/8" from the seam allowance leaving 1/4" beyond the stay stitching *(fig. 11-#2)*.

15. Turn the 1/4" seam allowance to the **right** side of the shell *(fig. 11-#3)* and straight stitch to hold in place *(fig. 11-#4)*.

16. Stitch the decorative threads to the right side of the neckline covering the 1/4" folded allowance *(fig. 12)*. Leave a 1/2" tail on the right side of the neckline.

17. On the left side of the neckline, continue stitching over the decorative threads for approximately 3". Flip this extension back to create a loop for the button. Stitch in place with a short straight stitch and zigzag. Trim away any excess portion of the loop *(fig. 13)*.

18. On the right side of the neckline, fold the decorative thread strip to the wrong side and press. Stitch in place with a short straight stitch and zigzag *(fig. 13)*.

19. Refer to the Shell General Directions steps 5, 6 and 7B with the following change in step 6:
    a. Leave 5" unstitched at the lower edge of each side seam. Clip through the seam allowance at the top of the 5". Trim and finish the stitched side seam with a zigzag or serge *(fig. 14)*.

20. Finish the bottom of the shell by turning the edge to the inside 1/4" and 1/4" again and top stitch in place *(fig. 15)*.

21. On each side of the shell, finish the edge by turning under 1/4" and 3/8" and top stitch in place *(fig. 16)*.

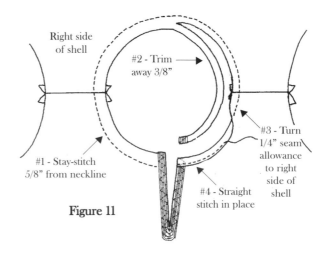

Figure 11

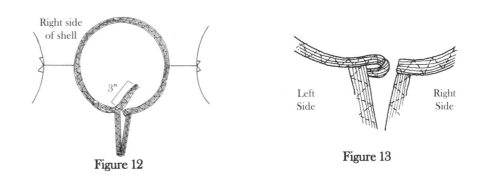

Figure 12

Figure 13

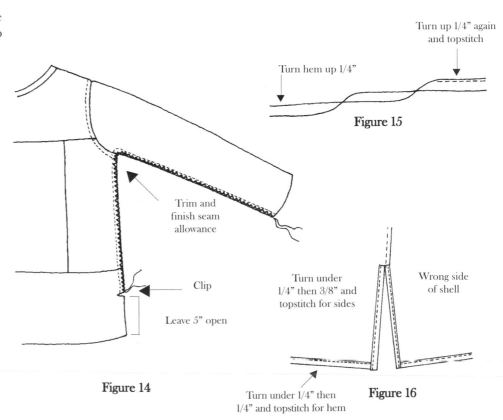

Figure 15

Figure 14

Figure 16

Elegant Netting Shell

Sue Pennington actually made a white "lace" shell using machine embroidery, shaped French lace insertion, and wide, embroidered English netting lace. Using imported 100% cotton netting for the foundation of the blouse, machine embroidery is stitched vertically in three places on the front of the blouse. Celtic lace-shaped ovals are found on the four rows of lace shaping; scallops in white French insertion are found at the bottom of the front treatment. Wide, white embroidered English lace edging is featured all the way around the bottom of the blouse as well as on the sleeves. White Swiss entredeux finishes the neckline. This shell is beautiful over a camisole with pants or a skirt, or over a body hugging slip dress.

- This shell was made with reference to the Shell General Directions, Round Neck, Short Sleeve Version found on page 6.

Supplies

- Refer to the Shell General Directions for fabric yardage
- 7" wide netting edging:
  XS - L   2-1/2 yards
  XL - 4XL   3-1/4 yards
- 3/4 yard of entredeux
- Water-soluble stabilizer (WSS)
- 9 yards of 1/2" lace insertion
- Wash-out marking pen
- Embroidery thread
- Thread to match lace
- One small button (1/2")
- Thread to match fabric
- Basic sewing supplies

Pattern Pieces

- Shell Front without dart – Round Neck Version
- Shell Back
- Shell Short Sleeve
- Lace Shaping and Scallops Template

Cutting the Pieces

- Cut a block of netting large enough for the shell front. Trace shell onto block.
- Cut one shell back on the fold
- Cut two short sleeves

* All seams are 5/8" unless otherwise noted. To finish seam, trim seam to 1/4" and overcast edge by machine or serger.

—Directions —

1. Draw a straight line down the center of the blouse front block with a wash-out marker. Draw 3 lines on each side of the center line, each 1-3/4" apart for a total of 7 lines. Additional lines totaling an odd number may be added to sizes larger than a medium.
2. Trace the lace shaping and scallops template. Place WSS behind the netting *(fig. 1)* and shape the lace on four of the lines (1, 3, 5, 7). Refer to the techniques for lace shaping. Stitch the lace in place with a small zigzag stitch.
3. Select an embroidery design that is about 1-1/4" wide and embroider the design on three of the lines (2, 4, 6) *(fig. 2)*.
4. Trace the shell front on the created block.

Elegant Netting Shell

Netting block for blouse front

1 2 3 4 5 6 7

Center front

Figure 1

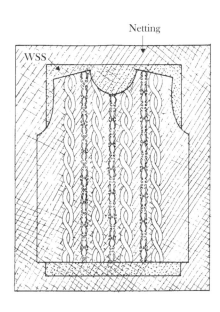

Netting

WSS

Figure 2

5. Lay the wide netting lace across the bottom of the blouse front and the blouse back with the finished edge of the netting on the hemline of the blouse. Using the template for the scallops, draw scallops across the top of the netting edge 6" up from the finished edge *(fig. 3)*. Refer to the techniques for lace shaping.

6. Stitch the side of the lace scallops closest to the netting lace trim using a small zigzag stitch *(fig. 4)*. Trim the excess netting lace edging on the right side of the fabric between the lace insertion and the netting *(fig. 5)*. Trim the excess shell netting fabric from behind the netting lace edging on the wrong side of the shell front *(fig. 6)*. Stitch the top of the lace scallops in place with a small zigzag *(fig. 6)*.

7. Lay the wide netting lace across the bottom of each sleeve with the finished edge of the netting on the hemline of the sleeve. Using the template for the scallops, draw scallops across the top of the netting edge 6" up from the finished edge *(fig. 7)*. Refer to the techniques for lace shaping.

8. Stitch the side of the lace scallops closest to the netting lace edging using a small zigzag stitch. Trim the excess netting lace edging on the right side of the fabric between the lace insertion and the netting *(fig. 8)*. Trim the excess netting fabric from behind the netting lace edging on the wrong side of the shell front. Stitch the top of the lace scallops in place with a small zigzag *(fig. 9)*.

9. Make an opening in the shell back as follows:
   a. Cut a 4" slit down the center back from the neck edge *(fig. 10)*.
   b. Open the slit and using a tiny close zigzag, overcast the cut edges *(fig. 11)*.

10. Place the front shell to the back shell at the shoulders, right sides together and stitch. Finish the seams *(fig. 12)*.

11. Refer to Beginning Lace Shaping Techniques, Entredeux to Flat Fabric, and attach entredeux to the neck edge of the shell using a 5/8" seam allowance and allowing 1/2" to extend at both sides of the shell back opening *(fig. 13)*. Trim away remaining tape edge.

12. Fold the extended ends flush with the back edge of the shell. Stitch in place by hand or machine.

13. Refer to the Shell General Directions, steps 5-6 and steps 9-10 to complete the shell.

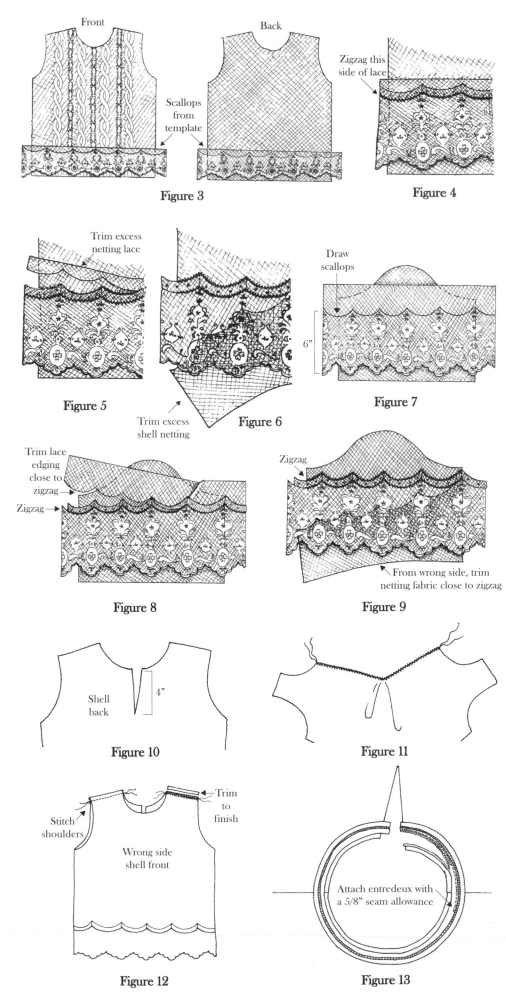

Figure 3

Figure 4

Figure 5

Figure 6

Figure 7

Figure 8

Figure 9

Figure 10

Figure 11

Figure 12

Figure 13

Triple Puffing Batiste Shell

A wide puffing panel is used on the front of this ecru Nelona Swiss batiste blouse which features a very interesting technique. Triple puffing is made by running rows of gathers in four places – on each outer edge of the center panel and two in the middle, dividing the panel into three sections. A fabric tube covers each of the two center gathering rows; decorative stitching holds each narrow tube in place. Little pearls have been stitched at points to emphasize the pretty decorative stitching. This beautiful shell was created by Pam Mahshie from Babylock.

- This shell was made with reference to the Shell General Directions, Round Neck, Long Sleeve Version found on page 6.

Supplies

- Refer to the Shell General Directions, Long Sleeve Version for the fabric requirements, adding 1/2 yard of fabric
- 2 yards of entredeux
- Decorative thread to match the fabric
- One small button (1/2")
- Thread to match the fabric
- Seed beads to match the fabric (optional)
- 1/2" bias tape maker
- Basic sewing supplies

Pattern Pieces

- Shell Front without dart–Round Neck Version
- Shell Back
- Shell Long Sleeve

Cutting the Pieces

- Cut a bias strip 2" wide by the neck measurement plus 1" for the bias neck facing
- Cut a strip from the selvage 1" wide by 8" long for the back neck opening
- Cut two rectangles 14" by 34" for each side of the shell front
- Cut two rectangles 8" by 45" for the puffing panel
- Cut two strips of fabric 1" by 45" for the tape strips
- Cut one shell back on the fold
- Cut two shell long sleeves

* All seams are 5/8" unless otherwise noted. To finish seam, trim seam to 1/4" and overcast edge by machine or serger.

—Directions—

1. With right sides together, stitch the two (8" x 45") rectangles together along one 8" side. Trim the seam allowance to 1/8" and zigzag the seam allowance. Press the seam to one side *(fig. 1)*.
2. Mark the lines on the rectangle for the puffing panel *(fig. 2)*.

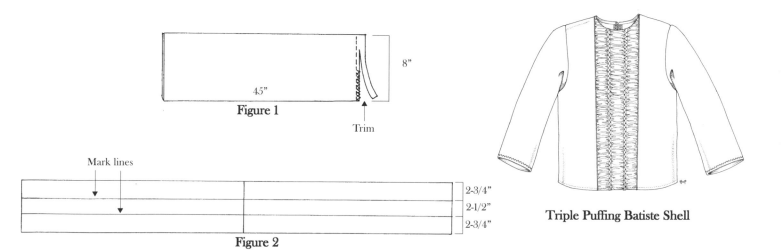

45"

8"

Figure 1

Trim

Mark lines

2-3/4"
2-1/2"
2-3/4"

Figure 2

Triple Puffing Batiste Shell

3. Stitch two gathering threads spaced 1/4" apart straddling each marked line and along each long side of the strip *(fig. 3)*.

4. Pull up the gathering threads until the piece has the fullness you like and still fits onto the size pattern front being constructed. You may have excess panel above and below the pattern area. The piece must maintain a rectangular shape *(fig. 4)*.

5. Following the instructions with your bias tape maker but using the 1" strips cut across the fabric, make two tape strips.

6. Place the two strips over the gathering threads as shown in figure 5 and pin in place.

7. Choose a decorative stitch no wider than 3/8" and stitch the design down the center of the tape strip attaching it to the puffing panel *(fig. 5)*.

8. Refer to Beginning French Sewing Techniques, Entredeux to Gathered Fabric and attach a strip of entredeux to each long side of the puffing panel. Place the entredeux between the two rows of gathering. Press the entredeux away from the puffing panel *(see fig. 6)*.

9. Refer to Beginning French Sewing Techniques, Entredeux to Flat Fabric and attach one 14" X 34" rectangle on each side of the puffing panel *(fig. 6)*. The puffing panel may be longer than the rectangle, but that is okay. Press the panel well.

10. Trace the shell front onto the completed panel *(fig. 7)*.

11. Straight stitch just inside the drawn line at the top and bottom of the puffing panel *(fig. 7)*.

12. Cut out the shell front along the drawn line.

13. Refer to the Shell General Directions and complete steps 1, 3 and 4 Round Neck Version – Bias Facing and steps 5-10.

14. You may stitch the same decorative stitch from the front of the puffing panel around the hem of the sleeves if desired.

15. Seed beads may be added to the decorative stitching if desired.

Gathering threads

Figure 3

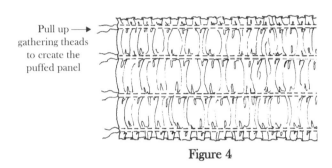

Pull up gathering theads to create the puffed panel

Figure 4

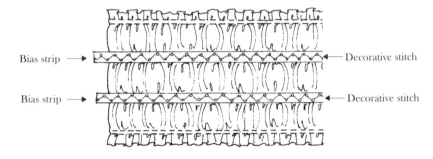

Bias strip → ← Decorative stitch

Bias strip → ← Decorative stitch

Figure 5

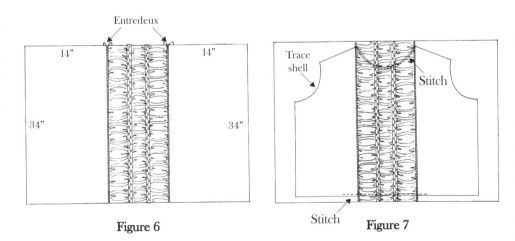

Entredeux

14"   14"

34"   34"

Figure 6

Trace shell

Stitch

Stitch   **Figure 7**

Scalloped Piping Linen Shell

Made of ecru handkerchief linen, this shell is tailored and very sophisticated. It would be the perfect shell to wear underneath almost any suit. The scalloped piping is made from folded bias strips stitched with either a shell or blanket stitch. The scalloped piping is featured around the bias binding on the neckline and at the top of the short-sleeved cuffs of the shell. The back placket on this blouse is terribly easy and pretty also. It is simply stitched with wing-needle triple entredeux stitch and sliced open! The neckline is closed with a button and loop. Connie Palmer, a Husqvarna/Viking educator, designed this elegant blouse.

- This shell was made with reference to the Shell General Directions found on page 6.

Supplies

Note: This particular shell should be made from fabric without a noticeable right and wrong side.

- Refer to the fabric requirements for the Shell
- One small button (1/2")
- Thread to match the fabric
- #100 wing or #120 universal needle
- One strip of heavy water-soluble stabilizer (WSS) (2" by 5")
- Fabric sealant
- Basic sewing supplies

* All seams are 5/8" unless otherwise noted. To finish seam, trim seam to 1/4" and overcast edge by machine or serger.

Pattern Pieces

- Shell Front without dart–Round Neck Version
- Shell Back
- Shell Short Sleeve

Cutting the Pieces

- Cut one shell front without dart on the fold. Trim 5/8" from the neckline of the front and back shell.
- Cut one shell back on the fold
- Cut two short sleeves
- Cut a bias strip 1-3/4" wide by the neck measurement plus 1" for the bias neck binding
- Cut bias strips 2" wide (you will need enough bias to go around the neckline and across the lower edge of each sleeve)
- Cut one bias strip 2-1/2" by 6" for the placket reinforcement

—Directions—

1. Stitch the bias together if necessary *(fig. 1)*. Fold bias in half with wrong sides together and press.
2. Sew a shell stitch or blanket stitch (L=3.0, W= 5.0) positioning it so that the swing of the stitch falls just off the edge of the fold *(fig. 2)*.
3. Trim seam allowance to 1/4" *(fig. 2)*. Lay the scalloped piping aside.

Scalloped Piping Linen Shell

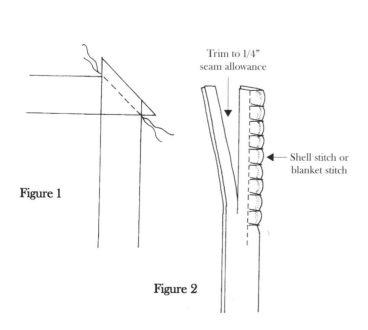

Trim to 1/4"
seam allowance

Shell stitch or
blanket stitch

Figure 1

Figure 2

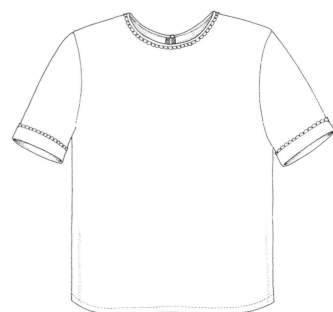

4. Make the hemstitched placket in the back as follows:
   a. Draw a 4" line down the center back from the neck edge.
   b. Place the 2-1/2" by 6" bias strip behind the line.
   c. Place the strip of heavyweight WSS behind the fabric strip.
   d. Starting on the left-hand side of the line, stitch a triple entredeux stitch using the #100 wing needle or the #120 universal needle letting the right-hand side of the pattern always touch the l ine. As you approach the bottom of the line engage the pattern stop button if available so that your machine will stop at the end of a pattern *(fig. 3)*.
   e. Pivot and stitch up the other side of the line, again letting the right-hand side of the pattern touch the line.
   f. When finished, remove as much stabilizer as possible and trim away any bias extending around the stitching.
   g. Carefully trim the fabric between the two lines of triple entredeux stitching stopping 1/4" from the bottom *(fig. 4)*.
   h. Fabric sealant may be used at the edges of the placket opening.

5. Place the front shell to the back shell at the shoulders, right sides together and stitch. Finish the seams.
6. Combine the bias neckband and the scalloped piping as follows:
   a. Fold the 1-3/4" wide bias in half with wrong sides together and press to crease *(fig. 5)*.
   b. Open bias out with the right side up.
   c. Place the scallop onto the bias strip lining up the straight stitch line of the scalloped bias with the fold of the bias strip *(fig. 6)*. Straight stitch the scalloped piping to the fold of the bias strip
   d. Refold the bias strip again matching the raw edges and allowing the scallop to extend from the fold of the bias *(fig. 7)*.
7. Place the strip to the neckline with the right side of the bias strip to the wrong side of the neckline and stitch together as shown in **figure 8**. Leave 1/2" extended on each side. Clip the seam allowance around the neckline.
8. Fold the bias up and over the seam to the right side of the shell, fold in the 1/2" extension and stitch in the ditch between the scallop and the bias *(fig. 9)*.

9. On the wrong side of each sleeve place a strip of scalloped piping matching the lower edge of the sleeve to the raw edges of the piping. Stitch a 1/4" seam *(fig. 10)*.
10. Fold the seam allowance towards the sleeve and press, allowing the scallop to extend beyond the end of the sleeve *(fig. 11)*.
11. Fold the hem of the sleeve to the right side and press, sandwiching the seam allowances between the sleeve the hem allowance. The scalloped piping will extend above the hem of the sleeve.
12. Stitch in the ditch between the scalloped piping and the fabric edge of the sleeve to secure the hem *(fig. 12)*.
13. Refer to the Shell General Directions, step 5, 6, 8, 9 and 10 to complete the shell.

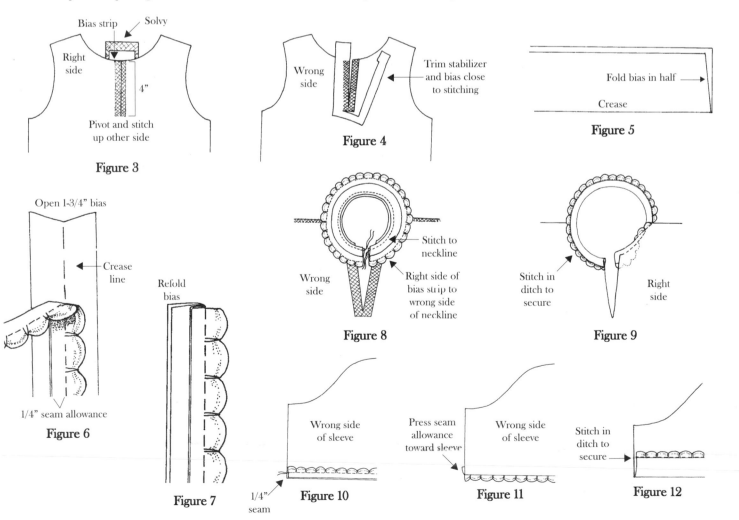

Figure 3

Figure 4

Figure 5

Figure 6

Figure 7

Figure 8

Figure 9

Figure 10

Figure 11

Figure 12

Ecru Linen Iris Shell

The V-neck version of the short-sleeved shell is beautiful with trims designed and stitched by Beverley Sheldrick. The shell is made of ecru handkerchief linen. Double-needle pintucks and silk ribbon embroidery by hand form the borders around the neckline as well as on the sleeves. Pale blue double-needle pintucks are found in square shapes as well as in double lines in between the square pintucks. There are pale blue, silk ribbon daisies in between the squares; tiny little purple stars are in between each daisy. Three brown and two gold iris flowers are stitched inside each square of blue pintucks. The irises have long green stems.

- This shell was made with reference to the Shell General Directions found on page 6.

Supplies

- Refer to the Shell General Directions, Short Sleeve Version for the fabric requirements; see note for V-neck version
- YLI silk ribbon (4mm) in the following colors:

Tan #139	2-1/2 yards
Gold #35	2 yards
Pale Blue #125	3 yards
Lavender Blue #117	1-1/2 yards

- #18 chenille or #22 tapestry needle
- 2.0/80 twin needle
- 7-groove pintuck foot
- Thread to match fabric
- Two spools of light blue thread to match silk ribbon #125 for pintucking
- Basic sewing supplies

Pattern Pieces

- Shell Front with dart—V-neck Version
- V-neck Facing Front
- V-neck Facing Back
- Shell Back
- Shell Short Sleeve
- Diamond, Medium Daisy, Tiny Daisy, Iris, and Sleeve Templates

Cutting the Pieces

- Refer to the layout for the Shell

- Mark the darts in the shell front

* All seams are 5/8" unless otherwise noted. To finish seam, trim seam to 1/4" and overcast edge by machine or serger.

—Directions—

1. Place the front shell to the back shell at the shoulders, right sides together and stitch. Finish the seams *(fig. 1)*.
2. Following the directions included with the template, draw a complete template on the blouse front and back and trace the pintuck lines *(fig. 2)*.
3. Place the sleeve embroidery template onto the lower portion of the sleeves and trace the pintuck lines *(fig. 3)*.
4. Stitch along the pintuck lines with a twin needle using the blue thread. DO NOT stitch the two pintuck lines where they pass behind a diamond. Pull the tails on the front of the stitching to the back and tie to secure.
5. Press the neckline and sleeves of the blouse and trace the embroidery designs.
6. Refer to the Iris and Daisy Embroidery Template and complete the embroidery designs referring to the embroidery techniques.
7. Refer to the Shell General Directions; step 4, V-neck Version with Facing and complete steps a – c.
8. Refer to the Shell General Directions, steps 5, 6, 7A and 8 to complete the shell. In step 7A the sleeve will be hemmed by hand.

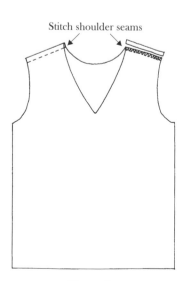

Figure 1

Stitch shoulder seams

Figure 2

Figure 3

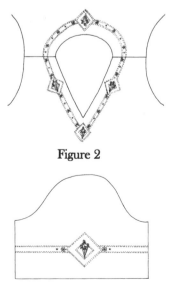

Ecru Linen Iris Shell

Blue Linen Sweet Pea/Foxglove Shell

The combination of lace shaping and silk ribbon embroidery makes this blouse, designed by Beverley Sheldrick, absolutely elegant. Little white lace ovals are found on each sleeve and on the center front of this blue handkerchief linen blouse. The lace ovals are stitched down with a wing-needle pinstitch using blue thread. We suggest using either a #100 wing needle or a #120 universal needle for the pinstitch. Two silk ribbon flowers - sweet pea and foxglove - are lovingly stitched by hand. The foxglove is stitched inside the lace oval in two shades of peach with green leaves. The sweet peas are on the outside of the oval in two shades of yellow and two shades of green. Stem-stitched green vines in embroidery floss surround the sweet peas.

- This shell was made with reference to the Shell General Directions found on page 6.

Supplies

- Refer to the Shell General Directions, Long Sleeve Version for the fabric requirements
- YLI silk ribbon in the following colors:

7mm	Green #18	2 yard
	Cream #156	1 yard
4mm	Yellow #13	1 yard
	Green #18	2 yard
	Dusty Pink #163	2 yard
	Med Pink #158	4 yards

- #18 chenille or #22 tapestry needle
- #8 crewel needle
- DMC floss #368 green
- #100 wing or #120 universal needle
- 1 yard of 3/4" lace insertion
- One small button (1/2")
- Thread to match fabric
- Tear-away stabilizer
- Basic sewing supplies

Pattern Pieces

- Shell Front with dart—Round Neck Version
- Shell Back
- Shell Long Sleeve
- Sweet Pea/Foxglove Embroidery Template

Cutting the Pieces

- Refer to the Shell General Directions and layout
- Cut a bias strip 2" wide by the neck measurement plus 1"
- Cut a strip from the selvage 1" wide by 8" long
- Mark the darts in the shell front

* All seams are 5/8" unless otherwise noted. To finish seam, trim seam to 1/4" and overcast edge by machine or serger.

—Directions—

1. Center the embroidery template on the shell front 4" down from the neck edge. Trace the template (**fig. 1**).
2. Center the embroidery template on each sleeve 5-1/2" down from the top edge of the sleeve. Trace the template (**fig. 2**).
3. Shape the lace insertion inside the lace template line on the shell front and the sleeves. Refer to lace shaping on page 79.
4. Place stabilizer behind the ovals and attach the lace insertion oval to the fabric using a #100 wing needle or a #120 universal needle and a pinstitch (L=2.0, W=2.0). Remove stabilizer and carefully trim the fabric from behind the lace insertion.
5. Refer to the Sweet Pea and Foxglove Template and complete the embroidery designs referring to the embroidery techniques. The embroidery will overlap the lace.
6. Refer to the Shell General Directions, steps 1-4, Round Neck Version – Bias Facing; steps 5, 6, and 7B, Long Sleeve Version; and steps 8 - 10 to complete the shell.

Figure 1

5-1/2" inches down from top edge of sleeve

Figure 2

Blue Linen SweetPea/Foxglove Shell

Pink Linen Fuchsia Shell

Made of pink handkerchief linen, this short sleeve shell has a border of three double-needle pintucks stitched to outline the "V" neckline. With Beverley Sheldrick's fuchsia flowers embroidered in silk ribbon, it almost seems to be alive with color. The fuchsia flowers are stitched in several shades of pink with the tops being lavender and lavender blue. Little blue drops extend from the bottom of each flower and green leaves and stems finish the designs. The three rows of double-needle pintucks are repeated around the sleeve bottoms along with three fuchsia flowers.

- This shell was made with reference to the Shell General Directions found on page 6.

Supplies

- Refer to the Shell General Directions, Short Sleeve Version for the fabric requirements; see note for V-neck version
- YLI silk ribbon (4mm) in the following colors:

Purple #117	1-1/2 yards
Lavender #102	1-1/2 yards
Raspberry #129	2-1/2 yards
Bright Pink #153	3 yards
Green #171	2 yards

- #18 chenille or #22 tapestry needle
- #8 crewel needle
- DMC floss #554
- 2.0/80 twin needle
- 7-groove pintuck foot
- Two spools of lightweight thread to match fabric for pintucking
- Basic sewing supplies

Pattern Pieces

- Shell Front with dart—V-neck Version
- V-neck Facing Front
- V-neck Facing Back
- Shell Back
- Shell Short Sleeve
- Fuchsia Embroidery Shoulder Template
- Fuschia Embroidery Sleeve Template

Cutting the Pieces

- Refer to the layout for the Shell
- Mark the darts in the shell front

* All seams are 5/8" unless otherwise noted. To finish seam, trim seam to 1/4" and overcast edge by machine or serger.

—Construction—

1. Place the blouse front and back together and stitch the shoulder seams. Trim and finish the seams *(fig. 1)*.
2. With a twin needle and pintuck foot stitch a pintuck 1" from the cut neckline of the blouse, beginning at the shoulder seam and stitching around the entire neck opening.
3. Stitch two more pintucks spaced approximately 1/8" apart *(fig. 2)*.
4. On each sleeve, stitch 3 rows of pintucks with the bottom row stitched 2-1/2" from the bottom cut edge of the sleeves *(fig. 3)*.
5. Position the embroidery on the left shoulder of the shell front just past the pintucking *(fig. 4)* and on each sleeve centered approximately 1" above the pintucking *(see fig. 3)*.
6. Refer to the Fuchsia Embroidery Template and complete the embroidery designs referring to the embroidery techniques.
7. Refer to the Shell General Directions, steps 2 and 4, V-Neck Version with Facing; steps 5-7A, Short Sleeve Version; and step 8 to complete the shell.

Pink Linen Fuchsia Shell

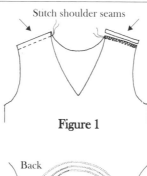

Stitch shoulder seams

Figure 1

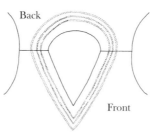

Back

Front

Figure 2

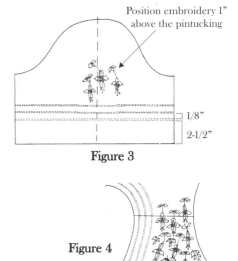

Position embroidery 1" above the pintucking

1/8"

2-1/2"

Figure 3

Figure 4

Jacobean Embroidered Shell

Designed by Kathy Neal, this ecru, handkerchief linen shell features Jacobean-type embroidery in many different shades. Kathy teaches hand embroidery on Martha's Sewing Room and all of her stitches for this series are stitched on this gorgeous shell with long sleeves. The stitches included in this design are chain, backstitch, stem, outline, satin, long and short, laid, raised stem, appliqué cord, herringbone, seeding, buttonhole, French knot and granito. The colors are wonderful and include purple, lavender, yellow, hot pink, gold, brown and several shades of green. Tiny touches of gold embroidery thread are used in the design.

- This shell was made with reference to the Shell General Directions, Round Neck, Long Sleeve Version found on page 6.

Supplies

- Refer to fabric requirements for Shell, Round Neck, Long Sleeve Version
- Embroidery floss; refer to stitch key with embroidery template
- #8 or #10 crewel needle for hand embroidery
- #100 wing or #120 universal needle
- One small button (1/2")
- Thread to match fabric
- Pencil or wash-out pen for tracing
- Basic sewing supplies

* All seams are 5/8" unless otherwise noted. To finish seam, trim seam to 1/4" and overcast edge by machine or serger.

Pattern Pieces

- Shell Long Sleeve
- Shell Front - Round Neck Version
- Shell Back
- Jacobean Embroidery Template

Cutting the Pieces

- Refer to the Shell layout for Round Neck, Long Sleeve
  NOTE: Do not cut out blouse front; follow instructions to trace pattern piece onto fabric and work embroidery, then cut out
- Cut a bias strip 1-3/4" wide by the neck measurement plus 1"
- Cut a strip from the selvage 1" wide by 8" long
- (Optional) Mark the darts

—Directions—

1. Position the embroidery template in the center front of the traced shell; the template will extend slightly into the seam allowance. Trace the template (*fig. 1*).
2. Embroider the design on the shell front. Wash to remove any remaining markings from embroidery; press dry. Replace the pattern piece over the embroidered fabric with the embroidery centered correctly. Cut out the shell front.
3. Refer to the Shell General Directions steps 1 – 10 to complete the shell, finishing the neck edge with the Bias Binding option in step 4. The sleeves are hemmed by hand in step 7b; the bottom edge is hemmed with a machine pinstitch using wing needle or large universal needle in step 8.
4. Optional: Add tiny tortoise shell rings, buttons, beads, or fringe to the sleeve edges; attach the trims by hand.

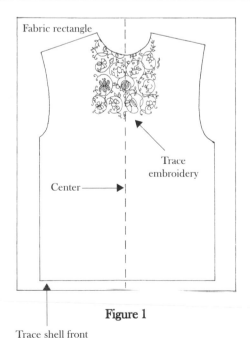

Fabric rectangle

Trace embroidery

Center

Figure 1

Trace shell front onto rectangle

Jacobean Embroidery Shell

Detail of Jacobean Embroidery Shell

Beginning French Sewing Techniques

Lace to Lace

Butt together and zigzag.
Suggested machine settings:
    Width 2-1/2, Length 1.

Gathered Lace to Entredeux

Trim one side of the entredeux.
Gather lace by pulling heading thread.
Butt together and zigzag.
Suggested Machine Settings:
    Width 2-1/2, Length 1-1/2.

Entredeux to Flat Fabric

Place fabric to entredeux, right sides together.
Stitch in the ditch with a regular straight stitch.
Trim seam allowance to 1/8".
Zigzag over the seam allowance.
Suggested Machine Settings:
    Width 2-1/2, Length 1-1/2.

Topstitch

(To be used after Entredeux to Flat or
    Gathered Fabric)
Turn seam down, away from the lace,
    entredeux, etc.
Tack in place using a zigzag.
Suggested Machine Settings:
    Width 1-1/2, Length 1-1/2.

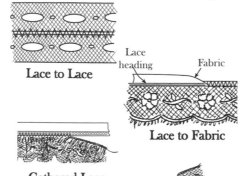

Lace to Lace

Lace to Fabric

Gathered Lace to Entredeux

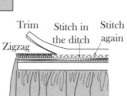

Lace to Entredeux

Trim — Stitch in the ditch — Zigzag

Entredeux to Flat Fabric

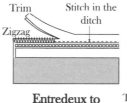

Trim — Stitch in the ditch — Stitch again — Zigzag

Entredeux to Gathered Fabric

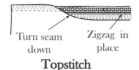

Turn seam down — Zigzag in place

Topstitch

Lace to Fabric

Place right sides together.
Fabric extends 1/8" from lace.
Zigzag off the edge and over the heading of
    the lace.
Suggested Machine Settings: Width 3-1/2,
    Length 1/2 to 1 (almost a satin stitch).

Lace to Entredeux

Trim batiste from one side of the entredeux.
Butt lace to entredeux and zigzag.
Suggested Machine Settings:
    Width 2-1/2, Length 1-1/2.

Entredeux to Gathered Fabric

Gather fabric using two gathering rows.
Place gathered fabric to entredeux, right sides
    together.
Stitch in the ditch with a regular straight stitch.
Stitch again 1/16" away from the first stitching.
Trim seam allowance to 1/8".
Zigzag over the seam allowance.
Suggested Machine Settings:
    Width 2-1/2, Length 1-1/2.

Making Piping

Bias strip

Stitch at an angle

Bias strip

Figure 1

Cord — Stitch — Bias strip — Press seam open

Figure 2

Supplies

- 1-1/4" wide bias strips
- Tiny cord
- Lightweight sewing thread to match the bias
- #70 universal needle
- Zipper foot or another foot allowing you to stitch close to the cord on piping

1. Piece the bias strips together to make one continual strip *(fig. 1)*. Trim the seam to 1/8" and press open.
2. Place the cording along the center of the strip on the wrong side and fold the fabric over the cording, matching the long edges of the fabric.
3. Use a zipper foot to straight stitch very close to the cording *(fig. 2)*.

Stipple Stitching

Supplies

- Basted quilt sandwich consisting of the top, batting and backing (Stipple stitching can be done without the backing.)
- Thread to match the backing if used
- Thread to match top or invisible thread for the needle
- Machine embroidery, Metafil, Metallica or Quilting needle, size 75 to 90
- Free Motion quilting or embroidery foot

Optional: Sewing aids that will help in moving the quilt sandwich

Machine Set-up

1. Set up the machine for free motion embroidery by lowering the feed dogs and placing the free-motion quilting or embroidery foot on the machine (see machine instruction manual).
2. Place a new needle in the machine.
3. Thread the needle with desired thread or invisible thread.
4. Use desired thread in the bobbin to match the backing.
5. The tension should be adjusted so the top thread does not show on the back and the bobbin thread should not be visible on the topside. Use a sample quilt sandwich to test and adjust as needed.

Rules for Free Motion Quilting

1. The feed dogs are always lowered or covered (see machine instruction manual).
2. The foot should be lowered before sewing. Some newer machines will not allow stitching with the foot in the up position, but older machines do not offer this. Lowering the presser foot engages the needle thread tension. If using free-motion stitching and a "bird's nest" is created on the wrong side, it usually indicates that the foot is not down OR that the top thread is not in the tension disks or take-up lever.
3. YOU are the stitch length in free motion stitching. The stitch length as indicated on the sewing machine does not come into play since YOU have to move the fabric (quilt sandwich).
4. Push the machine away from the edge of the table. This will allow the sewer to place the elbows or forearms on the machine bed or table. With the elbows up in the air, the shoulder, neck and arms become tired rather quickly. By placing the elbows down, the fingers can be placed on the quilt sandwich with the wrists up, allowing for easier controlled movement.
5. Position yourself directly in front of the needle.
6. Run the machine at a moderately fast, steady speed. The steady part of this statement is more important than the moderately fast. The speed of the machine must be adjusted to the speed of moving the fabric to create even-length stitches. If the needle breaks in free motion stitching, it is often because the speed of the sewing machine is too slow for the speed of moving the fabric. To create even-length stitches, practice stitching until even stitches are achieved.
7. Stipple stitching generally indicates that the stitches do not cross over each other, but are rather like the pieces of a puzzle. The curves are rounded, not squared. Stitch randomly to prevent a structured row look to the stitching. The stitching can be in a tight design or stitched in a looser design depending on the desired finished effect.
8. Begin near the middle and work out toward the sides.
9. Do not press on the quilt top too hard. This will make moving it more difficult and uneven.
10. Always tie-on and off at the beginning and end of stitching. This will prevent the stitches from raveling.

Stipple Stitching

NOTE: A template can be traced onto the fabric with a washout marker before beginning.

1. Position the quilt sandwich under the needle where the stitching will begin.
2. Sit comfortably directly in front of the needle with the elbows and fingers down and the wrists up.
3. Pull the bobbin thread to the right side by taking one complete stitch and pulling on the needle thread. Place the thread ends under your fingers and take several very tiny stitches to tie-on (**fig. 1**). Clip the thread ends.
4. Stitch at a moderately fast steady speed while moving the fabric in a smooth, even manner. There are many sewing aids that help in controlling the fabric although none are absolutely necessary: rubber finger tips, quilting gloves, hoops with rubber on the under sides (they look like a partial hoop – not enclosed in a circle – with handles on each side) and finger cots available at the drug store. Follow the directions on the product that you use. These sewing aids are not necessary, but they help in gripping the quilt sandwich so that it can be moved slowly.
5. Stitch in a random pattern that resembles puzzle pieces. Stippling may be stitched in a loose pattern (**fig. 2**) or a tight pattern (**fig. 3**). Stitching in vertical or horizontal rows becomes obvious. Change direction frequently, always rounding curves and keeping an even stitch length. It is important not to "paint yourself into a corner" and always leave an "escape route" when going into small areas. Practice with a pencil and paper to see how to stitch areas.

Figure 1

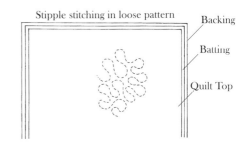

Stipple stitching in loose pattern

Backing

Batting

Quilt Top

Figure 2

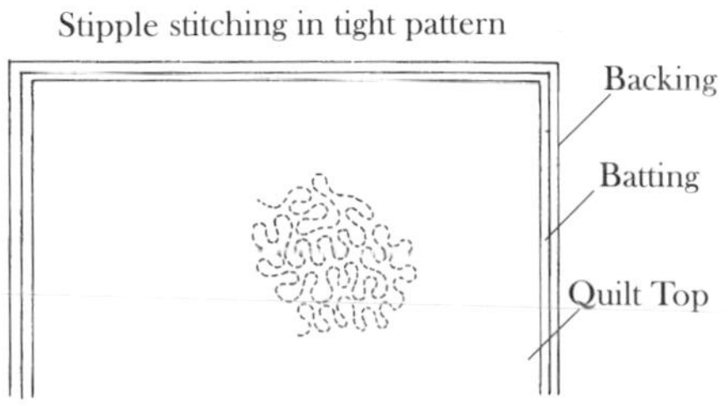

Stipple stitching in tight pattern

Backing

Batting

Quilt Top

Figure 3

Lace Shaping

Curves, Miters, Ovals and Diamonds

1. Trace the lace shape and miter lines onto the fabric with a wash-out pen or pencil (*see fig. 1*). Place the fabric on a padded surface, like a lace shaping board or ironing board. Note: If only one line is given for the template, shape the lace on the inside of the template. For scallops, shape the lace above the curve as shown (*fig. 1*). Scallops contain both curves and fold-back miters and are used in the illustrations.

2. *To shape a curve* - place the outer edge of the lace along the outer template line. Pin the lace to the template line by pushing glass head pins through the lace and fabric at an angle, into the padded surface. (Do Not use plastic head pins because they will melt.) Pin only along the outer edge; the inner edge will be loose and curvy (*see fig. 1*).

3. *To miter* - let the lace extend past the point (miter line) in a straight line. Pin the lace to the miter line at points A and B (*fig. 1*).

4. Fold the extended end of the lace back on top of itself. Leave the pin at B just as it is; remove the pin at A and replace it through both layers (*fig. 2*).

5. Continue to guide the lace along the next section of the template. Pin along the outer lace edge as before (*fig. 3*). Note: If part of the folded miter peeks out, just push it underneath the lace; it can be trimmed away later.

6. To shape the inner edge, slip the point of a pin under the top heading thread of the lace at the point of the miter, or at the center of a section between the miters. Pull the heading thread just until the lace is flat against the fabric (*fig. 4*).

7. Lightly starch and press as each section is shaped or after the entire design is pinned. The iron can be placed directly over the glass head pins; press until dry. Remove the pins and pin flat through the lace and fabric only, removing it from the padded surface (*fig. 5*).

8. Stitch the lace edge(s) to the fabric using one of the following methods:
   NOTE: The specific directions will indicate if one edge or both edges of the lace are to be stitched.
   • small zigzag (L=0.5 – 1.0, W=1.5 - 2.0) (*fig. 6*)
   • place tear-away stabilizer behind the design, use a large needle or wing needle and pinstitch (L=2.0 to 2.5), W=1.5 to 2.0). The straight side of the stitch should fall on the fabric while the "fingers" of the stitch will catch the lace (*fig. 7*).
   • place tear-away stabilizer behind the design, use a large needle or wing needle and an entredeux stitch (*fig. 8*)

9. Carefully trim the fabric from behind the lace, close to the stitching (*fig. 9*). Stitch along the lace miters with a small zigzag and trim the excess lace at the miters (*fig. 10*).

10. *To shape an oval* – Pin the outer edge of the lace along the template line. Overlap the ends of the lace by 1". Pull the heading threads along the inner edge of the lace (refer to step 6). Fold the top piece of lace under 1/2" (*fig. 11*). Lightly starch and press the oval and pin the lace to the fabric only (refer to step 7). Stitch as directed in the instructions (*refer to step 8*).

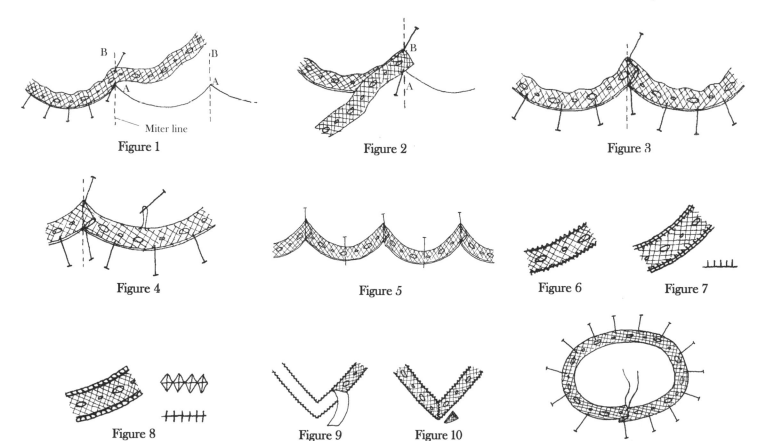

Figure 1   Figure 2   Figure 3

Figure 4   Figure 5   Figure 6   Figure 7

Figure 8   Figure 9   Figure 10   Figure 11

11. *To shape a diamond* – Place the lace inside the template with the outer edge of the lace along the template line. Allow the end of the lace to extend beyond the lower point placing pins at A and B *(fig. 12)*. Continue lace along the inside of the diamond, pinning at A and B again. To miter the corner, fold the lace back on itself. Remove the pin at B and re-pin through both layers of lace *(fig. 13)*. Continue shaping the lace along the template line *(fig. 14)*. When returning to the lower point, use the *fold back miter* method as follows: crisscross the ends of the lace at the miter line. Place pins through both layers of lace at B *(fig. 15)*. Remove the pin at A and fold the tail of the upper lace under to lie directly on top of the beginning lace tail. Repin at A *(fig. 16)*. Lightly starch and press the diamond and pin the lace to the fabric only *(refer to step 7)*. Stitch as directed in the instructions *(refer to step 8)*. Carefully trim the fabric from behind the lace *(refer to fig. 9)*. Stitch along the lace miters with a small zigzag and trim the excess lace at the miters *(refer to fig. 10)*. Figure 17 shows the lace diamond stitched to the fabric using a zigzag stitch.

Settings for Entredeux and Pinstitch

Bernina 180 E
Pinstitch
-100 wing needle or 100 universal
-Stitch #330 as is or L=2.5,W=2.5
Entredeux
-100 wing or 100 universal
-Stitch #701 as is or L=2.5, W=3.0

Pfaff 7570
Pinstitch
-100 wing or 100 universal
-Stitch #112, tension 3, twin needle button, L=3, W=4
Entredeux
-100 wing or 100 universal
-Stitch #132, L=5, W=3.5
-Stitch #113, L=2, W=4
-Stitch #114, L=2.5, W=3.5
-Stitch #115, L=3, W=3.5

Viking Husqvarna, Designer I and 1+
Pinstitch
-100 wing needle or 100 universal
-Stitch #D6, L=2.5 - 3, W=2 - 2.5
Entredeux
-100 wing needle or 100 universal
-Stitch #D7 (as is)

Elna CE20
Pinstitch
-100 wing needle or 100 universal
-Stitch #149, L=2.5, W=2.5
Entredeux
-100 wing needle or 100 universal
-Stitch #36, L=1.5, W=2.5

Singer XL - 1000
Pinstitch
-100 wing needle or 100 universal
-Screen #6, Stitch #7
-Medium or Small (width changes with the length)
Entredeux
-100 wing needle or 100 universal
-Screen #6, Stitch #8
-Medium or Small (width changes with the length)

Janome 10,000
Pinstitch
-100 wing needle or 100 universal
-Stitch #87 or #88, L=1.5 - 2.5, W=1.5-2.5
Entredeux
-100 wing needle or 100 universal
-Stitch #97, L=1.0, W=3.5

Brother ULT 2001
Pinstitch
-100 wing needle or 100 universal
-Screen #3, Stitch #4, L=3.0, W=2.5
Entredeux
-100 wing needle or 100 universal
-Screen #3, Stitch #8, L=2.5, W=3.0

Baby Lock, Esanté
Choose Decorative Stitch - Heirloom
Pinstitch
-100 wing needle or 100 universal
-Stitch #4 (as is)
Entredeux
-100 wing needle or 100 universal
-Stitch #5 (as is)

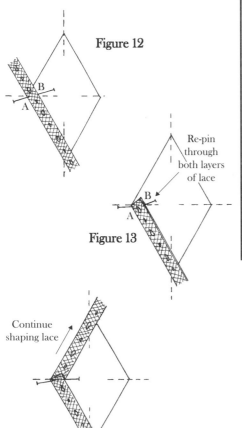

Figure 12

Re-pin through both layers of lace

Figure 13

Continue shaping lace

Figure 14

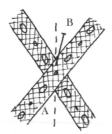

Figure 15

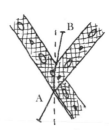

Figure 16

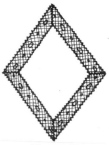

Figure 17

Free-Form Machine Appliqué

1. Hoop one layer of Sulky Soft'n Sheer™ stabilizer.
2. Spray KK2000™ onto a piece of Sulky Puffy Foam™ matched in color and size to the chosen design, and place it on the hooped stabilizer where the design will stitch out *(fig. 1)*.
3. Using decorative threads, embroider entire shoe design (or other design of your choice) *(fig. 1)*.
4. Pull away excess Puffy Foam™. Cut away the Soft'n Sheer™ close to the design. Use a wood burning tool or stencil cutter to carefully melt away excess Soft'n Sheer™ around the edges of the design. If any Puffy Foam™ peeks out between the stitches of the design, give the entire design a burst of steam from a hot iron held slightly above the Puffy Foam™ design to shrink the "pokies" into the stitching *(fig. 2)*.

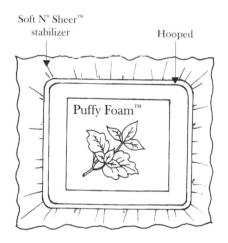

Soft N' Sheer™ stabilizer

Hooped

Puffy Foam™

Figure 1

Puffy Foam™ and stabilizer trimmed away from embroidery

Figure 2

Hand Embroidery Stitches

NOTE: Unless otherwise specified, work silk ribbon embroidery with tapestry or chenille needles; work floss embroidery with crewel or sharps needle.

Appliqué Cord

Cut a piece of Perle cotton or floss a little more than twice as long as design. Thread a tapestry needle with fine sewing thread. Lay perle cotton along one side of embroidery design and hold with thumb; begin at one side of design, not at end or point, because ends of thread must lie next to/on top of each other to finish. Begin stitching about 1/4 inch from end. Work one row of pinstitch over cording, turn around at end of design and place cording beside itself; work pinstitch along second side of cording. Finished stitch is a double row of cording with pinstitch along both sides, sharing center holes.

1. Bring needle up from wrong side and take a small backstitch to secure thread at point **a**. Take a 1/16-inch stitch from **a** to **b** *(fig. 1)*.
2. Take a 1/16-inch stitch from **a** to **c**, crossing under cord *(fig. 2)*.
3. Re-enter point **b**, crossing over cord. Point **b** will become new **a**; work again from **a** to **b** *(fig. 3)*.
4. Work from new **a** to **c** *(fig. 4)*.
5. Repeat stitch sequence to end of design line; small holes will be formed as points are stitched into multiple times *(fig. 5)*.
6. At end of line, turn cord around and make three to four **b-to-c** stitches. Point **b** will remain in same hole, but **c** will work around corner. Turn work over and continue **a-to-b**, **a-to-c** pattern in opposite direction. Turn final corner as described above and take a few more **a-to-b**, **a-to-c** stitches, then overlap ends of cord and finish stitching. Finish by weaving sewing thread through backstitches of design *(fig. 6)*. Carefully clip ends of perle cotton close to stitching on right side.

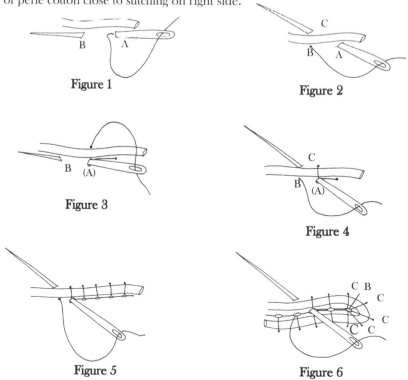

Figure 1

Figure 2

Figure 3

Figure 4

Figure 5

Figure 6

Buttonhole/Blanket Stitch

On the Fabric

1. Bring the needle up through the fabric at A. Pull the ribbon above and to the right of A and hold it in place with your thumb *(fig. 1)*.
2. Insert the needle in B and up through C in one stitch, keeping the ribbon under the needle *(fig. 2)*. Pull through.
3. C now becomes A and the sequence repeats. Notice that the stitch looks like a series of upside down "L's" *(fig. 3)*.

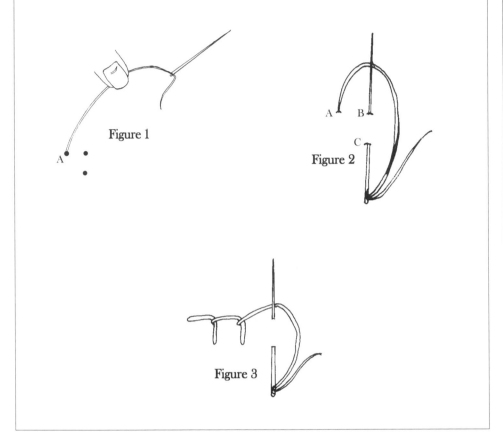

Fly Stitch

1. Come up at A. Insert the needle in the fabric at B, coming out of the fabric at C, making sure the loop of ribbon is below C *(fig. 1)*. Keep the needle on top of the loop of ribbon.
2. The length of the anchor stitch is determined by the length of the stitch taken between C and D. The floss or ribbon comes out of the fabric at C and the needle is inserted into the fabric at D. The longer the distance between C and D, the longer the anchor stitch. Gently pull the ribbon to the wrong side *(figs. 2 and 3)*.

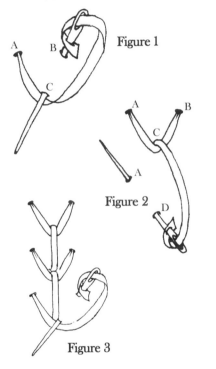

Chain Stitch

1. Bring the needle up through the fabric at A. Swing the floss or ribbon around in a loop and hold the loop with your thumb *(fig. 1)*.
2. While holding the loop, insert the needle back in at A and out through B in one stitch. Keep the needle and floss or ribbon going over the loop *(fig. 2)*.
3. Instead of inserting the needle to the other side like a lazy daisy, you will make another loop and insert the needle down, right beside B where you last came up, this will become a new A. In the same stitch bring the needle through B and pull *(fig. 3)*. Keep the needle over the loop.
4. Continue looping and stitching in an "A, B" – "A, B" sequence to the end of the design line.

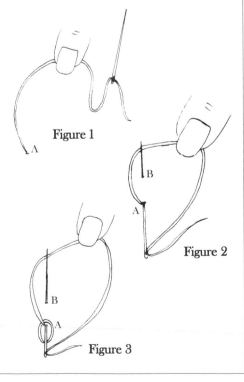

Japanese Ribbon Stitch

Use any size ribbon. Bring the needle up from under the fabric, loop it around and insert the needle down into the center of the ribbon a short distance in front of where the needle came up. Pull the ribbon so that the end curls in on itself loosely so that it does not disappear.

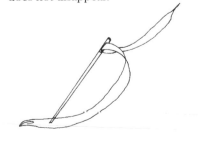

No-Fail French Knot

1. Bring the needle up through the fabric *(fig. 1)*.
2. Hold the needle horizontally with one hand and wrap the ribbon around the needle with the other hand *(fig. 2)*. If you are using a single strand of floss, one or two wraps will create a small knot. If you are making French knots with 2mm silk ribbon, the knot will be larger. The size of the knot varies with the number of strands of floss or the width of the silk ribbon being used.
3. While holding the tail of the ribbon to prevent it from unwinding off the needle, bring the needle up into a vertical position and insert it into the fabric just slightly beside where the needle came out of the fabric *(fig. 3)*. Pull the ribbon or floss gently through the fabric while holding the tail with the other hand.

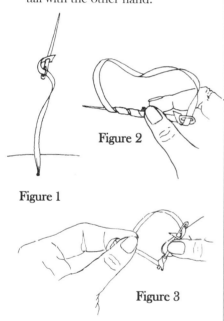

Figure 2

Figure 1

Figure 3

Satin Stitch

1. It generally helps if you have the area to be filled traced on the project so that you have two definite lines to guide and maintain the varying width of the stitch as it fills different shapes. Secure in embroidery hoop.
2. Begin at one end and work the needle from one side to the other, stacking the thread up just below and next to the previous stitch *(fig. 1)*. Continue this wrapping process, keeping the fabric secured and taut while the stitches are pulled with light tension so that the fabric will not tunnel.

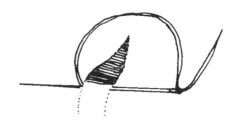

Lazy Daisy Stitch

1. Bring the needle up through the center point if you are stitching a flower, and up just next to a vine or flower for leaves *(fig. 1)*.
2. Insert the needle down into the same hole in which you came up. In the same stitch come through about 1/8" to 3/8" above that point *(fig. 2)*. Wrap the ribbon behind the needle and pull the ribbon through, keeping the ribbon from twisting *(fig. 3)*.
3. Insert the needle straight down into the same hole or very close to the same hole at the top of the loop *(fig. 4)*. Notice in the side view of figure 4 that the needle goes down underneath the ribbon loop. The top view of figure 4 shows that the stitch is straight and will anchor the ribbon loop in place.

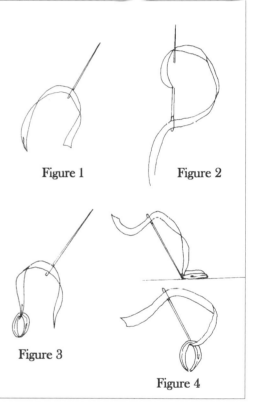

Figure 1   Figure 2

Figure 3

Figure 4

Pistil Stitch

1. Come up at A. Allow a short length of the ribbon to extend above A. Keep the ribbon flat and taut *(fig. 1)*.
2. Wrap the ribbon around the needle two times. Insert the needle at B, gently pull the wrapped ribbon down the needle until it rests against the fabric. Hold the ribbon taut as you pull the needle through the fabric forming a two-wrap French knot *(fig. 2)*.

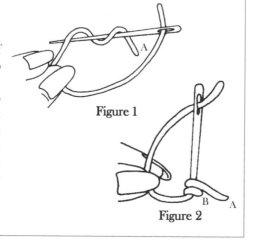

Figure 1

Figure 2

Running Stitch

Running stitch is a series of stitches run along the design line. Stitches should be as even as possible, with stitches on surface as long as back of stitches on wrong side of fabric. Work with an in-and-out motion of the needle tip; load several stitches onto the needle and then pull through.

Split Stitch

This stitch is used for outlining, stems and vines.

1. Trace the template on the fabric using a fabric marker or pencil. Take one stitch in the fabric (up at "A", down at "B") *(fig. 1)*.
2. Bring the needle to the front of the fabric "splitting" the first stitch *(fig. 2)*.
3. Repeat the stitching in this manner along the drawn line of the template *(fig. 3)*.

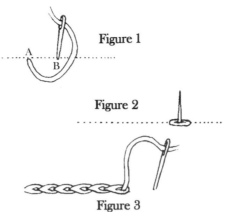

Figure 1

Figure 2

Figure 3

Straight Stitch

Simply bring the needle up from under the fabric and insert it down into the fabric a short distance in front of where the needle came up. It is an in-and-out stitch. Remember to pull the ribbon loosely for nice full stitches.

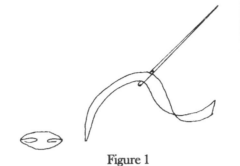

Figure 1

Figure 2

Stem/Outline Stitch

1. Come up from behind at A and go down into the fabric again at B **(see fig. 1)**. This is a little below the line. Come back up at C *(fig. 1)*. This is a little above the line. Keep the thread below the needle.
2. Go back down into the fabric at D and come up a little above the line at B *(fig. 2)*.
3. Continue working, always keeping the thread below the needle *(fig. 3)*.

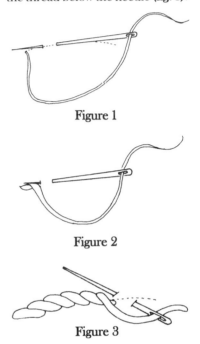

Figure 1

Figure 2

Figure 3

Couching

1. To start, bring the ribbon that is to be couched up through the fabric at an appropriate starting point and lay it flat in the direction you want it to be couched *(fig. 1)*.
2. Thread a needle with ribbon or floss in a matching or contrasting color. Bring the needle up just beside the ribbon at the starting point of the flat ribbon in figure 1. Take a stitch over the ribbon to the other side *(fig. 2)*. Continue wrapping the flat ribbon with the tack stitches, keeping them even in width and distance *(fig. 3)*.

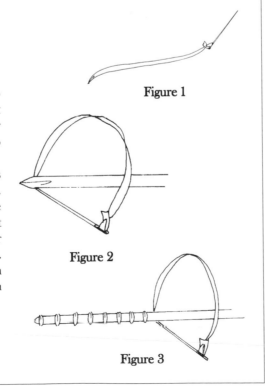

Figure 1

Figure 2

Figure 3

Herringbone Stitch

1. Work between two parallel lines. Bring needle to front at left end of one line. With thread to right, move diagonally to opposite line and pick up a small horizontal stitch along the line.
2. Move back to other side and pick up a small horizontal stitch with thread to right. Stitches may be spaced apart or taken close together, depending on the finished look you prefer.

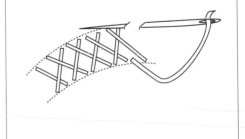

Medium Daisies

1. Stitch five petals from the center out with 4mm silk ribbon using a Japanese ribbon stitch. The stitches need to be approximately 1/4" long. Leave a small area in the center to place a French knot (**fig. 1**).
2. Stitch a small French knot in the center of each flower in the same color or contrasting floss (**fig. 1**).

Figure 1

Tiny Daisies

1. Stitch five petals from the outside of the daisy with 4mm silk ribbon or two strands of floss using a straight stitch. The stitches need to be approximately 1/16" to 1/8" long. Enter the same hole in the center of the daisy each time. Give the stitch a sharp tug before you take the next stitch. This will help to create a hole in the center of the daisy (**fig. 2**).

Figure 2

Simple Fuchsia

1. With a dark pink 4mm silk ribbon, straight stitch the bottom petals following the numbering system given in **figures 1a and 1b**.
2. Using 4mm ribbon in purple, work four Japanese ribbon stitches above the petals (**fig. 2**).
3. The stamens are pistol stitches. Work the center stitch first, making it twice as long as the two stitches worked on either side (**fig. 2**).

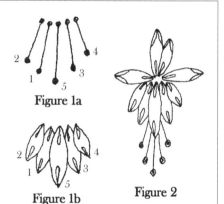

Figure 1a

Figure 1b

Figure 2

Sweet Pea & Vines

1. Draw a small oval at a slight angle lightly in pencil.
2. Thread a #18 chenille or #24 tapestry needle with 6" of 7mm cream silk ribbon. Bring to the front of the fabric at one end of the oval, leaving a small tail at the back.
3. Thread a sewing needle with 15" of cream machine thread.
4. Secure the silk ribbon tail at the back of the fabric.
5. Bring the needle and thread to the front of the fabric close to the silk ribbon.
6. With the machine thread, stitch 4 or 5 small whip stitches on the edge of the ribbon nearest the fabric (**fig. 1**). Pull up the thread and return the needle with the thread to the wrong side of the fabric to gather. Do not take ribbon to the back of fabric.
7. Repeat steps 5 and 6 working across the top of the oval (**fig. 2**).
8. Take the silk ribbon and the sewing thread to the back of the fabric behind the first "ruffle" (**fig. 3**).
9. Secure the tail of the silk ribbon with sewing thread. Clip away the excess silk ribbon.
10. In the center of the sweet pea, stitch two Japanese ribbon stitches in yellow 4mm silk ribbon (**fig. 4**).
11. Stitch three short Japanese ribbon stitches at the base of the flower in 4mm green ribbon to form the sepals (**fig. 4**).
12. The vine is worked with a backstitch using green embroidery floss.

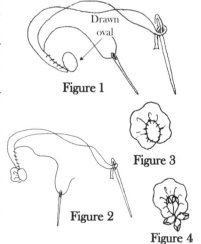

Drawn oval

Figure 1

Figure 2

Figure 3

Figure 4

Iris #1

1. Stitch the top of the iris with 4mm silk ribbon using a fly stitch with one side slightly lower than the other. We call this a tortured fly stitch. Leave the anchor stitch short and loose creating a small tunnel (**fig. 1**).
2. Bring the needle up again on the left hand side, placing it approximately 1/4" away.
3. Thread the ribbon through the tunnel left in step 1 and out the other side.
4. Take the needle to the back again, making the second side approximately the same size but at a different angle (**fig. 2**).
5. The stem and leaves are long straight stitches.

Iris #2

1. Stitch the top of the iris with 4 mm silk ribbon using a lazy daisy beginning and ending at the base of the iris bloom. Slightly elongate the anchor stitch at the top of the lazy daisy to create a point (**fig. 3**).
2. Bring the needle up again on the left hand side, placing it approximately 1/4" away.
3. Thread the ribbon through the bottom of the lazy daisy and out the other side.
4. Take the needle to the back again, making the second side approximately the same size but at a different angle (**fig. 4**).
5. The stem and leaves are long straight stitches.

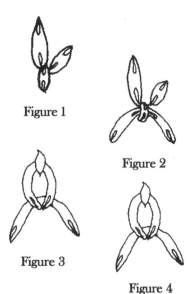

Figure 1

Figure 2

Figure 3

Figure 4

Long and Short

Work a foundation of split stitch along outline of shape to be filled; split stitch is indicated by dotted line in illustrations.)

1. Begin with a row of staggered stitches along outer edge of shape, stitching from inside to outside. Stitches should cover outline and lie side by side without overlapping; tuck needle under split stitch outline for a nice rounded edge *(fig. 1)*.

2. For second row, continue with staggered stitch lengths in a different shade or color. Each stitch should pierce stitch of previous row and cover 1/2 to 2/3 of previous stitch length *(fig. 2)*.

3. Continue with as many rows and colors as needled to fill shape. For last row, stitch from inside to outside and tuck needle under split stitch outline for a nice rounded edge *(fig. 3)*.

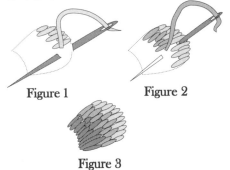

Figure 1   **Figure 2**

Figure 3

Eyelet

Make a small hole with stiletto or large needle. Anchor thread at edge of hole and bring needle to surface. Overcast edges of hole, always entering same hole and keeping overcast stitches an even size.

Backstitch

1. Bring needle to surface one stitch length from right end of line. Take needle down at end of line and bring tip of needle out one stitch length ahead of previous entry point *(fig. 1)*.

2. Continue by stitching "back" into hole of previous stitch and bringing tip of needle out one stitch length forward along line. Stitches butt head to toe *(fig. 2)*.

Figure 1

Figure 2

Seeding

Seeding is a simple filling stitch composed of small straight stitches placed at random angles *(fig. 1)*. The finer the working thread, the shorter the stitches should be to maintain a rounded appearance. to make larger stitches without gaining a long, skinny look, use a thicker thread or several strands of a finer one.

Figure 1

Granito

A granito is just a series of backstitches all worked into the same two holes; a rounded mound of thread will form. To keep the finished stitch round, begin with a short foundation stitch and stitch until the shape becomes round *(fig. 1)*.

Figure 1

Laid Stitches

1. Work a layer of parallel stitches across shape to be filled. Stitches are not satin stitches (crossing under fabric from edge to edge) but are laid: At end of stitch, come up beside the stitch a short distance away and go across top of shape in opposite direction to first stitch; refer to numbering in illustration *(fig. 1)*.

2. Work a second layer of laid stitches perpendicular to first layer. Second layer can be same color as first or contrast *(fig. 2)*.

3. To keep threads from moving on surface, couch each intersection with a tiny straight stitch over both threads *(fig. 3)*. Couching may be done with same or different color; sample shows gold metallic thread for couching in some sections.

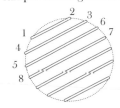

Figure 1

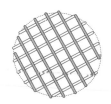

Figure 2

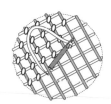

Figure 3

Leaf Stitch

1. Bring needle up just outside design line at tip of leaf. Insert needle one-third of the way down on vein line and bring tip of needle out to one side of tip, very close to where thread enters fabric *(fig. 1)*.
2. Insert needle back into vein line, one fabric thread behind first stitch, and bring tip out on opposite leaf edge, very near tip *(fig. 2)*.
3. Alternate stitches from side to side until leaf shape is filled *(fig. 3)*. It is important to keep stitches slanted moving back only one fabric thread with each stitch helps to maintain this slant *(fig. 3)*.
4. To end leaf, insert needle at base on vein line for last stitch *(fig. 4)*. Take thread to back and run under a few stitches on back to secure thread *(fig. 4)*.

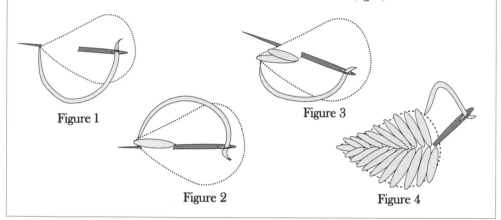

Figure 1

Figure 2

Figure 3

Figure 4

Raised Stem Band

1. Work a foundation of straight stitches that lie perpendicular to design lines *(fig. 1)*.
2. Work stem stitch over foundation stitches, picking up foundation thread only; do not stitch through fabric *(fig. 2)*. At end of row, tie off and begin again at original end.
3. Continue working stem stitch over foundation stitches until design area is completely filled in *(fig. 3)*.

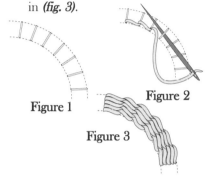

Figure 1

Figure 2

Figure 3

Foxgloves

1. Using one strand of floss, work 3 long straight stitches and secure at the back *(fig. 1)*.
2. Knot 12" of the lighter pink 4mm silk ribbon onto a #24 needle. Starting at the top of the straight stitch, work two French knots above the line approximately 1/16" apart *(fig. 1)*.
3. Following the diagram, work petals in long loose Japanese ribbon stitches, not pulling too tightly. You do not want a point at the end of the stitch *(fig. 2)*.
4. The leaves are Japanese ribbon stitches using green 7mm silk ribbon.

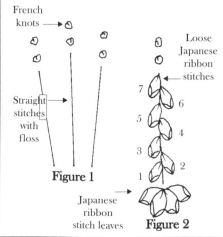

French knots →

Loose Japanese ribbon stitches

Straight stitches with floss

Figure 1

7
6
5
4
3
2
1

Japanese ribbon stitch leaves   Figure 2

Ruffled Fuchsia

1. Knot 6" of 4mm pink silk ribbon onto the needle. Bring it to the front of the left hand side of the position where the flower will be formed leaving a short tail on the back of the fabric.
2. Thread a sewing needle with 15" of pink machine thread and tie a tiny knot in the end of the thread. Tack the tail of the silk ribbon in step one to the back of the fabric. Bring the thread to the front at the same place as the silk ribbon.
3. Run a gathering stitch along the lower edge of the silk ribbon for 1-1/2" *(fig. 1)*. Gather this length up to 1 cm and stitch the ribbon in place to the right of the beginning point *(fig. 2)*.
4. Repeat this process in the opposite direction, coming back to the starting point *(fig. 3)*. Take the machine thread and ribbon to the back. Cut off the ribbon and secure the end to the back of the fabric.
5. Bring the machine thread to the front again and stitch ruffled ribbon in place.
6. Straight stitch the bottom petals using the same pink as for the ruffle, following the numbering system given in the *figure 4*.
7. Using 4mm ribbon in lavender, work four Japanese ribbon stitches above the ruffle, flipping and extending the one on each side *(fig. 5)*.
8. The stamens are pistil stitches. Work the center stitch first, making it twice as long as the two stitches worked on either side.
9. Leaves are Japanese ribbon stitches worked in 4mm green silk ribbon.
10. The stems are straight stitches with 2 strands of embroidery floss.

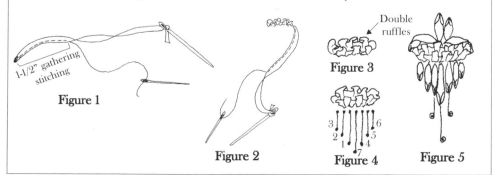

1-1/2" gathering stitching

Figure 1

Figure 2

Double ruffles

Figure 3

3 6
2 5
1 7 4

Figure 4

Figure 5

ABOUT
Martha Campbell Pullen, *Ph.D.*

Martha Campbell Pullen didn't invent heirloom sewing — the art of joining laces to create fabric has survived for centuries — but she and her fabulous staff can take some of the credit for turning this age-old art into a hobby that's approaching "all the rage" proportions.

Martha personally learned how to smock and French sew by machine over 20 years ago when she was making clothes for her baby daughter. She realized if she could be drawn in so passionately, other women could be as well.

Today, she fronts her own heirloom sewing empire, which grew out of a tiny shop in Huntsville, Alabama. In 1981, two months after opening that shop, she began importing laces and fabrics to sell mail-order, both wholesale and retail. Next, came Martha Pullen Schools of Art Fashion, which now attract more than 600 women to Huntsville twice a year. Their success prompted Pullen to venture out of her local market, conducting full scale Martha Pullen schools in Australia, England, Sweden, Canada, New Zealand and California. She has done mini-schools in almost every state in the United States.

An accomplished author, she has more than 38 books to her credit including four hardback manuals in excess of 400 pages. *You Can Make Money From Your Hobby* is published by Broadman and Holman, one of the world's largest Christian publishers. Her three latest books, *Martha's Quilts*, *Martha's Baby Doll Dessing*, and *Sew Kool 4 Kids*, are already best sellers.

Adding to that list of successes, and one of the projects of which she is most proud, is *Sew Beautiful*, a magazine she founded and began publishing in 1987. The publication focusing on heirloom and other classic sewing arts has an international following and distributes in excess of 100,000 copies bi-monthly. Eight years ago, she began sharing her love of heirloom sewing with public television audiences around the United States and Canada through her *Martha's Sewing Room* series (PBS).

To encourage heirloom sewn garments in cooler climates, Martha expanded the range of materials used from traditional batistes and other lightweight materials to wool challis, corduroys, flannels and home decorating fabrics. She has even come up with a name for these heirloom garments — love clothes.

"I call them 'love clothes' because I quickly realized that they are the special garments we make with love for the people we love," she explained. "With sewing, it almost seems that the love goes right from the machine or stitching needle into whatever we are making, especially where children are involved. It means so much more than just purchasing something ready made. Best of all, the classic, beautifully-sewn heirloom garments can carry that love from one generation to another."

Martha's Internet Machine Embroidery Club (IEC) has thousands of members who receive not only machine embroidery designs to be downloaded each month but also historical facts and poems. Her free weekly e-mail newsletter has a sewing tip, historic snippets from antique magazines, a personal letter from Martha, a scripture and a recipe. Go to *www.marthapullen.com* to sign up.

Annually, Martha presents "Martha's Sewing Market" at the Arlington Convention Center in Arlington, Texas and in Orlando at the Tupperware Convention Center. Her consumer exhibitions feature top international sewing instructors, more than 60 free class choices per day, a vendor arena, fashion shows, and displays. All of these activities are available after paying a low admission fee.

"Sewing makes memories that are passed on from generation to generation through the actual garments but also through the stitches learned," said Martha, who is on the road promoting the art of sewing many weeks out of every year.

A native of Scottsboro, Alabama, Martha is an internationally-known lecturer and teacher in the heirloom sewing field. After graduating with a degree in speech and English from the University of Alabama, she taught those subjects at almost every level of middle school and high school. Later, her studies led to a Ph.D. in educational administration and management from the University of Alabama. She has completed 30 hours of post doctoral work.

She has been named Huntsville/Madison County Chamber of Commerce Executive of the Year, the second woman in the history of the organization to receive this award. She has been a nominee for *Inc.* magazine's executive of the year. She is a member of Rotary International and Optimist International and has served on the board of directors of the Huntsville Symphony Orchestra and the Huntsville Community Ballet. She was named a national Daughter of Distinction of the Daughters of the American Revolution, the ninth person to receive this award. Recently, Martha was presented with the Golden Needle Award from the Schmetz Needle Company of Germany and Euro-notions. She has served on the board of directors of the Smocking Arts Guild of America and has presented workshops in French sewing by machine throughout the United States, Australia, England, Canada, Sweden and New Zealand. She is the wife of Joe Ross Pullen, a retired implant dentist and president of her company, mother of five and grandmother to twelve! An active member of her church, she also volunteers with the Southern Baptist International Mission Board in Africa, Jamaica, and Brazil.

To request a free Martha Pullen Company catalogue containing Martha Pullen products and publications, please write to:
Martha Pullen Company • 149 Old Big Cove Road • Brownsboro, AL 35741 • (256) 533-9586 • Fax (256) 533-9630
1-800-547-4176 • website – www.marthapullen.com • email – info@marthapullen.com